CORE
FACTS

The Strategy for Understandable and Teachable Christian Defense

Braxton Hunter

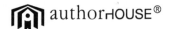 authorHOUSE®

AuthorHouse™ LLC
1663 Liberty Drive
Bloomington, IN 47403
www.authorhouse.com
Phone: 1-800-839-8640

Published by AuthorHouse 02/25/2014

ISBN: 978-1-4918-4311-6 (sc)
ISBN: 978-1-4918-4309-3 (hc)
ISBN: 978-1-4918-4310-9 (e)

Library of Congress Control Number: 2014902242

Contents

For Michele Clime, my surrogate big sister
already in the arms of her Savior

INTRODUCTION

Uneducated, ignorant, behind the times; these are the labels that Christians often receive from coworkers, classmates and friends. As a young pastor, I was bombarded with this sort of language. Even though I had been firm in my faith, the bluntness and glib certainty of critics was unnerving. I began to doubt. After all, some of the most intelligent people I knew were the very ones hurling these objections at the faith I was preaching. I decided to begin researching the old arguments for the existence of God that I had heard when I was a teenager in a freshman philosophy class. Searching library bookshelves, I poured over the modern classics on the evidence for the resurrection of Jesus. After wrestling with these weighty issues for about four years, I realized a peace that I could not explain.

Uneducated? How laughable this assertion became. It wasn't the leading philosophers and physicists who brushed off the evidence for Christianity. It was the uninformed students. Internet trolls made up the majority of the atheist scoffers. I learned quickly that while the most knowledgeable specialists in the relevant fields are not all necessarily believers, most of them take the evidence seriously and enjoy engaging in honest discussions about it. In short, the skeptics I knew were wrong. The Christian God exists, and there is powerful reason to believe.

Once I began visiting other churches I realized that these evidences for the truth of the Christian message could be used not only to bolster the faith of believers, but also in witnessing to others. Many times, I presented the arguments and cases for the faith to crowds of unbelievers. In time, I learned of their embrace of the truth. In terms of leading doubters to faith in Christ, discovering these evidences amounted to striking gold. The problem was that almost no one was using them in this way. The only time anyone talked about this sort of thing was in philosophy class. Some Christians had read through Christian apologetics books and enjoyed talking about the material with other congregants, but there was a disconnect when it came to unbelievers. They needed to hear these things and the church wasn't sharing them. I went looking for the reasons why.

First, most of our personal evangelism training material is designed around the assumption that unbelievers already accept that there is a heaven and hell, that Jesus is the way of salvation and almost everything else. After reading the key evangelistic question of one of the popular personal evangelism training resources, Christian apologist, Norman Geisler, pointed this out saying,

> One of the reasons that our old evangelistic techniques don't work anymore whether it's *Evangelism Explosion* or *Campus Crusade*, or *Way of the Master*, is because people don't believe the prerequisites. Notice the prerequisites of that question. He believes there's a heaven, a hell, a God who has revealed himself . . . people don't believe that anymore. The vast majority in our country no longer believe that. That means it will no longer work on the vast majority of people.[1]

It became clear to me that there needed to be an evangelistic training resource that made the classical case for the truth of the Christian message understandable and easy to remember.

In 2008 I began hammering out a method like this and decided to start using it in my own ministry. The result was C.O.R.E. F.A.C.T.S. Since that time, I have used the method to present the same faithful arguments for the Christian faith that classical apologists have grown to favor in a memorable way. I have used it for evangelism in formal public debates, private conversations, internet radio discussions

---

[1]   Geisler, Norman, "Trinity 2008 Commencement Address Part 3," (youtube. com/watch?v=z0l_mS-a0l8) Internet. Accessed on 21 March, 2012.

and while preaching in churches. It has served me well and proved invaluable as my signature method.

This work will explain the arguments involved and how to use them for the affirmation of your own faith or to reach others for Christ. If you are an unbeliever, I ask you to read this work with an open mind. You might even ask the God you do not believe in to speak to your mind and heart during this study. The book is designed in such a way as to be helpful and accessible to all who read it.

Chapter one explains the evidence for God's existence from the fact that the universe must have had a "Cause" for its own existence. This is a famous cosmological argument. The second chapter lays out the phenomenal "Order" of the world in which we live. Why is the universe so seemingly well designed? This is a presentation of a teleological (design) argument for God's existence. Chapter three will consider the "Rules" that the universe seems to have for human morality. Isn't it interesting that people everywhere have an awareness that certain things are good and bad, right and wrong? Many readers will recognize this as a moral argument. In the fourth chapter, the case will be made that individuals can have an immediate "Experience" of God if they are open to the evidence. This sets the stage for us to consider the resurrection of Jesus.

Leaving the arguments for God's existence, chapter five will be a demonstration that Jesus' wounds on the cross were "Fatal." In it, we will consider the evidence that Jesus really did die by Roman crucifixion. After all, if we are going to claim that he rose from the dead, then it needs to be demonstrated that he really was, in fact, dead. From there, the investigation will lead us, in the sixth chapter, to consider the claims that Jesus "Appeared" to others after his death. Chapter seven will be an examination of the level of "Commitment" that the disciples had to the message of the resurrection. This will open the door to the "Testimony" of early Christians about this whole matter in chapter nine. Finally, chapter ten will be an explanation of the logical conclusion one should draw on the basis of these Core Facts. Namely, Jesus is the way of "**S**alvation."

You may notice that this is a two-step approach. The evidences represented by the acronym "C.O.R.E." are all related to the existence of God. However, this material doesn't specify that the God being argued for is the one true God of Christian Scripture. This is why the evidences represented by the acronym "F.A.C.T.S." show that Jesus is the one true God who has revealed himself in creation. In this way it will not be unreasonable to conclude that Jesus was raised by God from the dead since God's existence is demonstrated in the first half of the case. In other words, if God exists as the creator of the universe, then raising Jesus from the dead is no problem for him.

CORE MOMENT

Pay attention to these "CORE MOMENT" boxes. If you are a beginner or just need a little clarification, these simplified explanations will help. As long as you watch the boxes, you'll finish with a good foundation.

In each chapter I explain and respond to the most frequent objections to these evidences. I take it as my self-designated responsibility to equip readers with the best defense possible. In some cases, the responses to objections take up more space than the explanations of the arguments themselves. I also conclude each chapter with a presentation on how a trainer or facilitator might teach the material to a class of learners. Those closing sections are also a great help for any reader who is struggling and in need of a simplified explanation. If you find that the material covered in the objections is too complex, just skip to the next section of the chapter. Just to ensure that I have given readers the best chance of success, an appendix is included which explains a conversational method of defending the faith. It is filled with extra evidence. The second appendix provides an easy reference outline of the C.O.R.E. F.A.C.T.S. so that they can be remembered and shared with others. Finally, I have included a debate that I had in 2009 in which I used the C.O.R.E. F.A.C.T.S. method. For the reader who wishes to see how the case handles the rigorous scrutiny of a well versed skeptic, the debate will be enlightening. It is my hope that all readers will close this book with an understanding of why we believe what we believe and how to defend it before a questioning world.

The C.O.R.E. F.A.C.T.S. acrostic is designed in such a way that the primary arguments can be easily remembered. Because the two words that form the acrostic are separate in what they seek to demonstrate, they can be broken up and used separately. That is to say, if an individual already believes in God but sees no reason to accept the truth of the resurrection of Jesus, the Christian can simply bypass C.O.R.E. and focus entirely on the F.A.C.T.S. of the resurrection of Jesus. Perhaps someone would embrace Christianity if only they thought it were possible that God existed. In such a case, one might focus on the C.O.R.E. arguments. This flexibility is one of the strengths of the method. It should also be said that I have no desire to replace other evangelistic strategies. Instead, C.O.R.E. F.A.C.T.S. can be used in symphony with existing resources to satisfy the need to defend the truths that they present. The goal is 21st century evangelism.

Though most Christians are completely unaware of, or apathetic toward them, there are powerful reasons to believe. This book will explain them. Ready yourself for the journey, open your mind, roll back the uncertainty, loose the chains of doubt, ignite the fires of discovery and engage the evidence.

CHAPTER I

C

THE UNIVERSE HAD A CAUSE

In the beginning God created the heavens and the earth.
—*Genesis 1:1*

Introduction

Of all the arguments for the existence of God, it is my belief that a proper form of a cosmological argument is the strongest deathblow to atheism which can be brought from the arena of the natural human mind. While it is certainly the case that certain types of evidences and formal arguments will be persuasive for individuals of varying backgrounds and personality types, this family of arguments strikes many thinkers as uniquely clinching. Frank Tipler writes,

> When I began my career as a cosmologist some twenty years ago, I was a convinced atheist. I never in my wildest dreams imagined that one day I would be writing a book purporting to show that the central claims of Judeo-Christian theology are in fact true, that these claims are straightforward deductions of the laws of physics as we now understand them. I have been forced into these conclusions by the inexorable logic of my own special branch of physics.[2]

---

[2]   Tipler, Frank, *The Physics of Immortality*, (New York, NY: Doubleday, 1994), Preface.

It is likely because of this that classical apologists have reserved a special position of prominence to their versions of cosmological arguments. While certain scientific formulations, like design arguments, are remarkably appropriate to the sorts of concerns modern unbelievers have regarding theism, the philosophically and scientifically potent thrust of this kind of argument allows it to bypass many of the common objections posed by the 21st century naturalist. Moreover, it is precisely because of this that much of what the apologist argues with a cosmological case is immediately accessible to the common man. Certainly some of the philosophical principles involved will require definition, but the overarching premises and metaphysical principles are rooted in facts that can be reviewed in the arena of the listener's own mind. That is to say, very little prerequisite knowledge of physics or science is necessary for the average thinker to ascertain the logic employed by the apologist.

CORE MOMENT

This first argument might sound overly complicated, but actually anyone can learn how to use it. You don't need to have an advanced degree. If you're a 13 year old boy or a 60 year old woman, you can understand and use this evidence if you'll only commit to understanding it.

This is no trivial point. Pastors are reporting that one of the primary reasons Christians avoid the study of Christian defense is because they find the subjects involved to be overly-complicated. If local ministers could learn and explain these arguments in a compelling and digestible way, then the task of evangelism would move forward considerably. Most importantly, God's people would have made great strides toward the mandate of 1 Peter 3:15 to be ready to give an answer to anyone who asks a reason for their hope.

For the purposes of this work, I find it to be the most prudent expenditure of space to focus on one specific form of a cosmological argument rather than present what would amount to a museum of historical uses and formulations. This rendering has been chosen because of its ease of explanation and relevance for current debates. What will come first is a formal stating of the argument and explanation of how it is used. Secondly, we will discuss common objections brought by atheists and agnostics. Finally, we will attempt to show how the argument can be presented in a teaching format for digestion by lay church members. As this is the first of the theistic arguments to be discussed in this volume, it is vital to remind the reader that a skilled Christian defender will not merely use any theistic argument singularly. These arguments lead listeners to the realization that there is a God, but not to the firmly specific fact that he is the God of Christian Scripture. For such purposes, the resurrection case of chapters five, six, seven, eight and nine, should be made. Let me make one final statement.

This argument, represented by "C." is the most technical part of C.O.R.E. F.A.C.T.S. You may find yourself struggling at first. However, a careful consideration of what this chapter explains is truly powerful. Remember, if it becomes too complex, you can always take a look at the simplified explanation toward the end of the chapter in the section, "Transitioning the Formal Argument for the Layman." Nevertheless, you will be challenged, but the understanding you will have at the end of this first chapter will be satisfying. It is my favorite argument for the existence of God.

The Cosmological Argument: Stating the Case

Stating this case will require at least two steps, broadly speaking. First, it will be necessary to state a formal cosmological argument. Then, it will become appropriate to provide the logical implications of the argument, which allow thinkers to arrive at God's existence. The formal argument will merely point to a first uncaused cause of the universe. This, coupled with the explanation from simple scientific data, will lead to the clear conclusion that God must be this uncaused CAUSE.

The Formal Argument

The formal argument is often stated in the form of an Aristotelian syllogism. Syllogisms like this are comprised of two premises which lead to an undeniable conclusion. An example of this is as follows:

1. If today is Sunday, the library is closed.
2. Today is Sunday.
3. Therefore, the library is closed.[3]

If both premises (1) and (2) are true, then it follows necessarily that the conclusion, ". . . the library is closed." is true also. Thus, if issue is to be taken with the argument, then critics must demonstrate the falsity of either premise (1), or premise (2). For example, one might point out that the library in question is actually open every third Sunday of the month. This would represent a challenge to premise (1). They may demonstrate that the individual making the argument is confused and "today" is actually Saturday. Such would be an attack on premise number (2). However, if both premises (1) and (2) are true, then there is no way to escape the truth of the conclusion (3).

---

[3] Craig, William Lane & Moreland, J.P., *Philosophical Foundations for a Christian Worldview*, (Downers Grove, IL: Intervarsity Press, 2003), 28.

CORE MOMENT

Don't worry! I'm only explaining this so you know how arguments work. If you're a beginner, you don't really need to know this stuff. Philosophical terms and arguments look scary, but I'll break down the evidence itself without them.

Careful consideration must be given to the premises of an argument. A good argument will be both formally and informally valid. In order for it to be a formally valid argument, it must contain a conclusion that flows from the premises in accordance with the rules of logic. To be informally valid means that it contains no logical fallacies. Moreover, a good argument will contain premises which are plausible. That is to say, each premise is more likely to be true than it is to be false.[4] The formal cosmological argument that follows is formally and informally valid and contains premises that are plausible.

Here is how a common cosmological argument is stated:

1. Everything that begins to exist must have a <u>CAUSE</u> for its existence.
2. The universe began to exist.
3. Therefore the universe must have a <u>CAUSE</u> for its existence.

With this argument in mind one can see how the argument stands up to the standards we have just discussed.

Premises (1) and (2) are both plausible. They are more likely to be true than false. There are no apparent logical fallacies and the conclusion follows directly from the premises. The strength of the argument becomes clear upon the consideration that the only way to challenge it is to attempt a demonstration that premise (1) or premise (2) is false. We will interact with examples of these challenges when

---

[4]   Nash, Ronald, *Faith & Reason*, (Grand Rapids, MI: Zondervan, 1988), 95.

we discuss objections to the argument later in the chapter. For now, notice the position into which this argument places readers. They now see that the universe must have a cause for its existence. Nevertheless, we have not narrowed our field of vision such that it is clear what that cause must have been. In order to accomplish this feat, we must draw implications from some simple scientific principles. This will move us to the second broad step of the case.

CORE MOMENT

All we're saying in this formal argument is that something or someone had to CAUSE the world to come into existence. That's really it! The only reason for all the philosophical talk is that the argument is set up to handle objections.

Implications of the formal argument

To put it simply, if the universe has a cause for its existence, it must be one of two very general types of causes. It is either a natural cause, or it is a supernatural cause. Now when the term supernatural is used here, I am only referring to a cause that is not natural. Yet, if the coming into being of all of the natural world is what is on the table, then a natural cause simply will not do. After all, whatever natural cause one might credit with the creation of the universe would itself be a part of the natural order (the universe) and thus be a part of that which requires explanation. The cause, then, must be a supernatural one simply because all of nature cannot cause itself to come into being. So what does this mean?

All that is in the universe can be categorized under three headings, namely, time, space and matter/energy. These categories comprise the natural world. Though it may seem strange to imagine, outside of the universe time itself does not exist. This is not only the conclusion of theologians. Modern physicists agree with this claim. Furthermore, matter does not exist. When we say matter we are also referring to energy. Finally, space itself does not exist outside of the physical universe. Extraordinarily, the space that you inhabit while reading this book, the space that the milky way exists in, and even the space of every distant galaxy did not exist outside of the physical universe. This means that whatever caused time, space and matter to come into being must be something that is not in any of those categories.

CORE MOMENT

It's simpler than it sounds. Time, space and matter make up nature. What we are trying to figure out is what or who caused nature to come into existence. So the cause can't be anything in time, space or made of matter. Those things are nature. Nature is what we are trying to explain. Our cause has to be timeless, spaceless and not material.

A simple explanation of why this is so will help to clarify the case. If standing before you were a beautiful painting and I asked you what caused this painting to come into existence, how would you respond? Clearly, you would say that some skilled artist was the evident cause. I might, however, retort that the red dot in the upper right quadrant of the painting caused its existence. Perhaps the blue line at the bottom was the cause. This would strike you as absurd. Nothing in the painting could have caused the existence of the painting. Undeniably, things in the painting cannot cause the painting to exist precisely because they are a part of what was created. Similarly, time, space nor matter could cause the universe to come into existence because they are a part of what was created.

Thus, the cause of the universe must not be in time. It must, instead, be eternal. The cause cannot be material, but non-material. Whatever brought the universe into being must not occupy space, it must be spaceless. For these reasons, it is clear that the cause of the universe must be an eternal, non-material, spaceless something. Yet, if the argument only brought us this far we would surely be at a loss. What we need to determine is what sorts of things fall into those categories.

There are a few things besides God which would fit the bill. Abstract items, such as the very laws of logic themselves exist in this way as do mathematical principles. In other words, the idea that two plus two equals four would still be true even if there were no material objects to add. The law of non-contradiction that (a) cannot be (a) and (not a) at the same time and in the same way would still be true and existent if there were no "things" to describe. However, these items do not have what philosophers refer to as "causal powers." Simply put, they cannot *do* anything. For obvious reasons, they cannot bring anything into existence. What is necessary is something that falls into these categories but also has "causal powers." The only possible feature that accomplishes this is a bodiless *mind*. Clearly, minds have causal powers.

CORE MOMENT

Don't let the talk of math and laws of logic distract you. The point is that the only possible cause that is timeless, spaceless and not made of matter is a mind without a body. This is what Scripture teaches that God is (John 4:24).

From these clear implications, the universe must have a cause which is an eternal, spaceless, non-material mind. At the very least, this is what any orthodox Christian theist means when he refers to God. The cosmological argument that I have just set forth may require some review in order to fully appreciate, but it should be understandable to any thinking person who is willing to devote a little time and consideration to it. The truths that spring forth from these revelations are the sorts of things that have caused agnostics and atheists to say very theistic things. This well known quote from Robert Jastrow is a fine example:

> For the scientist who has lived by his faith in the power of reason, the story ends like a bad dream. He has scaled the mountains of ignorance; he is about to conquer the highest peak; as he pulls himself over the final rock, he is greeted by a band of theologians who have been sitting there for centuries.[5]

Objections to Premise 1

CORE MOMENT

These objections can get kind of technical. If you're a beginner, it might be a good idea to just focus on the actual argument we've covered so far. You can always come back to these objections once you've grown in your understanding a little more. If you think you're ready then keep reading. Just don't get discouraged if it's tough at first.

---

5   Jastrow, Robert, *God and the Astronomers*, (New York, NY: W.W. Norton, 1978), 116.

Doesn't quantum physics demonstrate that some things come to exist without a cause?

Over the past several years quantum physics has become the bright hope for naturalists who wish to remove God as the uncaused cause of the universe. Many have tried to postulate unconventional theories of time and space in order to reject the truth of premise (2), but recently quantum theorists have challenged premise (1) by asserting that it actually is possible that the universe came to exist, uncaused out of absolutely nothing. Most famously, theoretical physicist, Stephen Hawking, argued the following,

> Because gravity shapes space and time, it allows space-time to be locally stable but globally unstable. On the scale of the entire universe, the positive energy of the matter can be balanced by the negative gravitational energy, and so there is no restriction on the creation of whole universes. Because there is a law like gravity, the universe can and will create itself from nothing in the manner described in Chapter 6. Spontaneous creation is the reason there is something rather than nothing, why the universe exists, why we exist. It is not necessary to invoke God to light the blue torch and set the universe going.[6]

However, there are a number of problematic statements found in Hawking's comments which demonstrate a misunderstanding of the cosmological argument.

First, Hawking argues that because gravity has the power to shape space-time, universes will result. This shows that he understands the cosmological argument to be aimed only at the material aspects of the physical universe. That is to say, the tangible substance that we think of when we usually refer to physicality. Nevertheless, what the

---

[6]   Hawking, Stephen, *The Grand Design*, (New York, NY: Bantam, 2010), 180.

argument addresses in actuality is the totality of the contents and make up of the universe itself. Gravity is an aspect of the physical universe which itself is contingent and requires explanation.

Similarly, the existence of positive and negative energy requires explanation. Hawking sees the energy of the universe to have a balance of zero because of the positive versus negative energy. However, this is not zero in fact. Zero in fact would be no positive and no negative energy in existence at all.

Finally, the physicist seems to be unaware that the cosmological argument addresses the existence of space and time. In order for there to be a balance of energy, gravity and any sort of activity at all, there must exist space for these interactions to occur within. Yet, the existence of space itself is the existence of something. What Hawking calls nothing is not actually nothing.

What his work amounts to is a redefinition of terms so that a victory for naturalism can be claimed. What Hawking refers to as zero energy is not actually zero energy, what he calls nothing isn't nothing and what he thinks is an explanation of why the universe exists is actually his explanation of why it turned out the *way* that it did. This evokes the words of philosopher Thomas Nagel. He writes,

> The existence of our universe might be explained by scientific cosmology, but such an explanation would still have to refer to features of some larger reality that contained or gave rise to it. A scientific explanation of the Big Bang would not be an explanation of why there was something rather than nothing, because it would have to refer to something from which that event arose. This something, or anything else cited in a further scientific explanation of it, would then have to be included in the universe whose existence we are looking for an explanation of when we ask

why there is anything at all. This is a question that remains after all possible scientific questions have been answered.[7]

Alternative quantum arguments which seek to demonstrate that something can come from nothing make the same misstep. The fact that a quantum physicist may say that a given particle came into existence uncaused does not mean that it did. It means that one cannot determine what the cause was. This also depends somewhat on what one means by causality. If space exists for quantum events to occur in, then the space itself is a type of cause. For example, if I place a book on a shelf and ask what is causing the book to be suspended in the air, the natural answer is that the shelf is causing it to be suspended. Space is the shelf that causes quantum events to be possible.

Ultimately, none of this demonstrates that something can come to exist uncaused out of nothing. It is a semantic appeal to how we understand certain terms. These objections misunderstand the cosmological argument. Worse still, the very items that need explanation are admittedly contingent and in need of a CAUSE.

CORE MOMENT

The atheist is trying to say that the universe could have come to exist without a cause because a field of science called quantum physics has shown that some things do happen without a cause. The problem is that quantum physics hasn't shown this and there is a huge difference between something in the universe happening and the whole universe itself coming into existence from nothing.

---

[7] Nagel, Thomas, *Secular Philosophy and the Religious Temperment* (New York, NY, Oxford University Press: 2009), 28

Who created God?

One of the more common objections to premise (1) is actually a commission of the *"tu quoque"* fallacy. What this means is that the critic simply claims that the proponent of a given argument has the same problem that he is asserting the critic has. It would be like responding to the charge, "You lied about cheating on the exam" by saying, "Well, you've lied to me about things too." Rather than responding to the charge, one points out that their opponent has the same problem. However, even in light of this obvious fallacy, there is a clear defense.

What is important to note, is that premise (1) claims "Everything that BEGINS to exist must have a cause for its existence." Clearly, if something did not begin, then it does not need a cause. Since God is timeless and eternal, he does not require a cause. Only and all temporal things begin and stop existing. More clearly, time is necessary for beginnings and endings. Thus, if God exists in eternity, where time is not, then he does not require a cause for his existence. Remember, this is not a cop-out. This is a proper category placement. If God is timeless, then temporal terms cannot be meaningfully ascribed to him. Thus, the objection fails.

CORE MOMENT

God has no beginning, so God doesn't need a cause. The only kind of things that need causes are things that start to happen or exist.

How do we know that the universe is not the one temporal thing that needs no cause?

In order for this to be maintained, one would have to demonstrate two things. First, if such a claim is meant to be considered plausible then it would have to be shown that anything has ever come into existence uncaused out of nothing. Second, it would have to be explained how this is even philosophically possible. Neither of these two items has ever been successfully accomplished.

Some philosophers have set forth an object lesson for understanding why this is untenable in the following way. Imagine finding an orb of some kind in a field. You might not know what it is or where it came from, but you can be certain that it had a cause of some kind. Now imagine that the orb is as large as the field itself. Clearly, all that was true about the smaller orb is still true of the larger orb. The fact that it is now much larger does not explain its existence. It still needs a cause. Think of an orb as large as a planet. Does it need a cause? Clearly it does. What about an orb the size of the universe itself? Does this orb now need a cause? The objector now claims that it does not. Yet, nothing changed about the orb except for its magnificent size. It still requires a cause.

What about "the composition fallacy?"

One makes the mistake of the composition fallacy when he asserts that if something is true of the individual parts of something, then it must be true of the whole. For example, someone might mistakenly argue the following:

1. Dogs are made of atoms.
2. Atoms cannot be seen by the naked eye.
3. Therefore, dogs cannot be seen by the naked eye.

Clearly, this is false.

Atheists sometimes argue that theists make the same mistake. The fact that everything in the physical universe requires a cause does not necessarily mean that the universe itself requires a cause. However, this is merely a more firm presentation of the former objection. The second item mentioned above still needs to be satisfied in order for this objection to stand.

Objection to Premise 2

CORE MOMENT

If the universe has just always existed and had no beginning, then it doesn't need a cause (such as God). That's why some atheists argue that the universe has always existed. Don't be fooled. It hasn't always existed. We'll see why.

What if the universe is infinite in its existence?

This objection challenges the truth of premise (2) directly. Many thinkers have argued that if premise (1) is true but premise (2) is false, then there is no good reason to conclude that the universe requires a cause. On this view, the universe had no beginning. Instead, history stretches infinitely into the past. However, the 21st century is a difficult time for advocates of such a view to make their cases. Though it was not the case a century ago, modern science has arrived at a sense of clarity regarding the beginning of the universe. That is to say, that it did happen.

As far back as 1993, George Smoot claimed, "The question of 'the beginning' is as inescapable for cosmologists as it is for theologians."[8] His compatriots have echoed this sentiment with a resounding declaration that according to the best scientific evidence available, the universe did indeed begin to exist a finite time ago. Alexander Vilenkin writes,

> It is said that an argument is what convinces reasonable men and a proof is what it takes to convince even an unreasonable man. With the proof now in place, cosmologists can no longer hide behind the possibility of a past-eternal universe. There is no escape: they have to face the problem of a cosmic beginning.[9]

Such certainty has come for a couple of reasons. First, in 1964, Arno Penzias and Robert Wilson discovered what is known as the "cosmic background radiation" of the universe. This is a field of radiation unaffiliated with any specific star or body and is uniformly dispersed throughout the universe. It represents clear evidence of a cosmic event that took place in and via the origin of the universe itself.

Arno Penzias explained, "Astronomy leads us to a unique event, a universe which was created out of nothing, one with the very delicate balance needed to provide exactly the conditions required to permit life, and one which has an underlying (one might say 'supernatural') plan."[10] Clearer scientific support for the truth of premise (2) would be difficult to find.

Second, in 1925, Edwin Hubble demonstrated that the universe is in a state of expansion by documenting the speeds of distant

---

[8] Smoot, George, *Wrinkles in Time*, (New York, NY: William Morrow & Co. 1993), 189.

[9] Vilenkin, Alexander, *Many Worlds in One*, (New York, NY: Hill & Wang, 2006), 176.

[10] Penzias, Arno, *Cosmos, Bios and Theos*, (La Salle, IL: Open Court, 1992 ed.), 83.

galaxies compared to their distances from the earth. If the universe is expanding from a central point, then it follows that it began to expand. If one considers the reverse of the expansion it becomes clear that the logical origin was an incredibly small and dense point outside of and before which there was literally nothing. As some of today's top physicists explain,

> The universe began from a state of infinite density . . . Space and time were created in that event and so was all the matter in the universe. It is not meaningful to ask what happened before [the event]; it is like asking what is north of the north pole. Similarly, it is not sensible to ask where the [event] took place. The point-universe was not an object isolated in space, it was the entire universe, and so it can only be that [the event] happened everywhere.[11]

The conclusion which demands to be made is that this infinitely dense universe would continually have grown smaller (if it is viewed in the reverse) to the point of non-existence. Thus, we have a second scientific argument for the beginning of the universe. For both of these reasons, it is not scientifically feasible to conclude that the universe existed infinitely into the past. However, there is powerful evidence from philosophy that counts against an infinite universe.

CORE MOMENT

All we have shown in our response so far is that everything we observe in science indicates that the universe began to exist. Get ready! The rest of our response is the most complicated point of the whole book. Just stay with it!

---

[11] Gott, Richard J., et. al., "Will the Universe Expand Forever?," (Scientific American, March 1976), 65.

The greatest philosophical argument against the claim that the universe existed infinitely into the past is known as the impossibility of an infinite regression of causal events. What this argument claims is that the universe simply cannot have existed infinitely into the past because this would necessitate an actual infinite number of events throughout its history. If there are an actual infinite number of events, then "today" would never have come simply because it would be impossible to cross an actually infinite amount of time.

In order to understand this claim, one must have an understanding of what is meant by the phrase *actual infinite*. A *potential infinite* represents an idea which exists only conceptually. For example, we can imagine that time may continue into the future infinitely. This means that it will never end. We can likewise imagine that if we were to move toward a given point and only move half of the distance each time, we could make an infinite number of moves because there will always be another half-distance we could traverse, no matter how small. These are *potential infinites*, but not *actual infinites*. A simpler way of saying this is that infinity only really exists as a concept, but it does not actually exist in reality. We use the term infinite in common parlance in improper ways quite often. One may refer to an infinite number of grains of sand on the beach, but there really is not an infinite number. The number may be monstrous and nearly inconceivably high, but there is a number we may ascribe to it. An *actual infinite* means that there simply is no such number. *Actual infinites* do not exist in reality.

A variety of analogies have been advanced by philosophers to illustrate why the universe could not have an actually infinite number of points in its history. If there are an infinite number of what we would call years stretching back infinitely into the past, then there would be odd numbered years and even numbered years. Now imagine if every odd numbered year was removed so that only the even numbered years were left. How many years would there now be? There would still be an infinite number of years in the history of the universe because infinity minus half of infinity would still equal infinity. Thus, time could have never arrived at today because it would never have been able to traverse an actually infinite number of points.

Another analogy involves a hypothetical library with an infinite number of books. If all of the books in the infinite library were either black or red so that all even numbered books were red and all odd numbered books were black, imagine removing all of the red books. Now how many books would be left? There would still be an infinite number of books, they would just all be black books. To put it as simply as possible, no matter how many points in time past in the history of the universe, time would never have arrived at today because no matter how much time has passed there is still an infinite amount of time yet to overcome. Thus, the universe cannot extend infinitely into the past because it would involve an infinite regression of time.[12]

It is important to mention that there are arguments from science claiming that the universe could have existed prior to the event which caused the expansion and background wave radiation, but even if this were so, it would not escape the truth revealed by this philosophical argument. Thus, premise (2) holds true. The universe began to exist a finite time ago.

CORE MOMENT

Just relax! All that philosophical talk is just a complicated way of saying that if there was no beginning for time then we would never have gotten to this point in time. That means the universe had a beginning.

---

[12] Christian apologist, J.P. Moreland, has used this analogy in many of his debates and lectures.

Objections to the God Conclusion

Isn't this a commission of the "god of the gaps" fallacy?

It is quite common for skeptics to demand that in spite of the truths of premise (1) and premise (2), God is not the proper explanation for the cause of the universe. They claim that theists are guilty of committing the "god of the gaps" fallacy in positing God as the cause. The "god of the gaps" fallacy occurs when some god is given as the explanation of some phenomenon, not because there is any positive reason to believe God is the causal agent, but rather because it is unclear what the cause is. Illustrating this, some ancient religions argued that lightning must be an act of a god simply because they had no knowledge of what caused lightning. The criticism is that theists are committing the "god of the gaps" fallacy because they simply don't know what *is* the cause of the universe.

Nevertheless, when it comes to the cosmological argument, theists are doing no such thing. It is not the case that we have no positive evidence for God as the cause. In fact, the evidence points squarely to God's existence as the cause. There simply is nothing else in existence that is eternal, spaceless, non-material and has causal powers. Only a mind independent of a body would qualify. Therefore the "god of the gaps" fallacy does not apply. What would be necessary to demonstrate the fallacy would be an explanation of any other philosophically possible cause besides God.

Do we have any evidence of a mind that is not attached to a physical body?

On the heels of the last objection, some skeptics demand that we have no examples of a mind that is independent of a physical body. Because of this, it must be *ad hoc* for theists to claim that a mind independent of such a body could possibly exist as the cause of the universe. Two responses must be made. First, there is nothing internally incoherent in the idea of a mind independent of a body. Second, the cosmological argument itself serves as an argument for the existence of such a mind. If it is the case that the cause of the universe must be eternal, spaceless, non-material and retain causal powers, then it must also have the power of the will in order to decide to create the universe from nothing.

Isn't it possible that science will one day provide a natural cause for the universe?

The problem with this question is threefold. First, it represents unbridled skepticism. Rather than a "god of the gaps" fallacy, this is something like a "naturalism of the gaps." We don't know what the cause is, so it must be some natural cause that we will later understand. Second, because nature is what requires an outside cause, the supernatural is the only possible explanation. Third, this is not something that requires future explanation. The God hypothesis is already a satisfactory answer. As with any scientific hypothesis, scientists should always be open to the testing of this claim, but as it stands, God is the best explanation. However, philosophically I see God as the only explanation.

Transitioning the Formal Argument for the Layman

It should be apparent by this point that this is a deeply philosophical argument with deeply philosophical objections. The average reader may have trouble grasping certain aspects of the cosmological argument and for that reason it becomes necessary to provide a simpler explanation. What will follow is an attempt to present the argument in such a way that it will be understandable to a wide demographic without losing its potency. Undeniably, this means the removal of terminology which demands prerequisite knowledge.

Nevertheless, it is my belief that the basic ideas attached to the argument are easy to grasp and the key premises already held by most.

The apologist or facilitator should begin by asking the students to reflect on the question of why anything exists instead of nothing. Why is there anything here at all? This lays the foundation for the overall subject of the argument, which is the existence of the universe. If students have never really considered this question, then this should lead them into the arena of consideration which will be their training ground for digesting and hopefully using the argument.

From here, the discussion of the formal argument can commence. One might ask, "Can you think of anything that has ever started to happen or began to exist that wasn't caused by something else?" I often point out that from a very early age, children are aware of the idea that everything that happens is caused by something else. For example, when my daughter was nine months old I tossed her a ball to see if she had developed enough dexterity to catch it. Unfortunately, the ball bounced softly off of her head and she tumbled over. I realized very quickly that this is not the best experiment to do with a nine month old. Still, when she sat herself back up she began to look around. What she was doing was an investigation to determine what caused her to fall over. More impressive still, when she saw the ball she began to look around for what caused the ball to fly through the air, causing her in turn to fall down. At an age when she was not even able to formulate an intelligible word, she was already aware that everything that begins to happen must have a cause. Simple personal analogies like this one help students to establish the principles on which premise (1) is based.

For premise (2) it is helpful to point out the scientific data that establishes the truth that the universe began to exist. Quoting some of the authorities mentioned above will demonstrate to the student the truth of the premise. Occasionally, some students will object to the authorities mentioned because the student knows that the mechanism by which these scientists claim the universe began to exist was the Big

Bang. They have been trained by some pastors and creationists that the Big Bang is an elaborate part of the argument for the truth of evolution and so they have a knee-jerk reaction to any mention of such concepts. The point to drive home is that however one believes the universe came into existence, scientists have arrived at the belief that it did in fact come into existence. This is all that is required to demonstrate to skeptics the truth of premise (2). Thus, if an individual has an issue with the mention of the Big Bang, it is reasonable to point out that when using the argument the student need not abandon his own beliefs about what was the mechanism God used. To firm up the truth of premise (2), one could attempt to explain the infinite regression argument, but this may be digging too deep for some students. After all, the evidence already supplied will likely be enough to demonstrate how the argument works.

At this point the students are ready to put these two simple truths together and realize that the universe must have had a cause. As was stated before, the next step is to show them what the cause must have been, as well as what it could not have been. This too can be accomplished using some simple explanation and analogy.

Explaining the Implications of the Argument for the Layman

What could have been this cause that brought the universe into existence? The facilitator might first explain that something cannot cause itself to come into existence. Then, to illustrate, he might ask, "Did you decide to be born, or did your parents cause you to come into existence by conceiving you?" Clearly, the latter is correct. So the universe could not have caused itself to come into existence. Continuing, he might add, "If by 'universe' we mean all of nature, then whatever caused the universe must be something outside of nature, or 'supernatural.'" At this point an analogy, like the painting we mentioned earlier, is a nice fit. Sometimes I use digitally animated movies to make the point. I ask whether the star character of the film caused the movie to come into existence. Naturally, they laugh and admit that such an idea is impossible. Instead, a skilled computer animator, as well as a lot of other film-makers, caused the movie to come into existence. But, why is this the case? Obviously, this is so because the lead character is a part of the film. The existence of the film and everything in it are what we are trying to explain. Therefore, the cause must be something outside of the film.

So, when we consider the explanation of the existence of the whole universe, we cannot explain it by appealing to anything in it. Of what is the universe made? It is made of time, space and matter. Thus, as was the case with the film and painting, whatever caused the universe cannot fall into any of these categories. It must be an eternal (timeless), spaceless and non-material cause. And it had to have a mind in order to create the universe. This sounds quite a bit like God doesn't it?

When you strip the argument down to its bare bones, this is what is revealed. Moreover, it really isn't that difficult to explain or accept. A careful mind will also notice that almost all of this is immediately accessible to the student. No matter their academic background, the simply stated cosmological argument is made up of ideas and truths that most people already accept about the nature of reality. Clearly, the presentation is stronger and more enjoyable when more personal illustrations and examples are added.

Conclusion

The cosmological argument is one of the strongest arguments for the existence of God. It is not incredibly difficult to understand, although defending it may require a knowledge of some of the deep issues discussed in the objections. It is structured in such a way that any critic must show a fatal flaw in premise (1), premise (2), or the implications which spring forth from the formal argument. Having examined the challenges atheists have made against the premises and their conclusion, it should be apparent how strong the logic is. Moreover, it can be creatively explained to the average individual without much difficulty. For all of these reasons, the cosmological argument, discussed here, is a powerful evidence for the existence of God.

Questions

1. Why does the "C." in C.O.R.E. F.A.C.T.S. stand for *Cause*?
2. Why must the cause be outside of time and space, and not made of matter?
3. How would you respond if someone asks, "who made God?"
4. Why must the universe have had a cause for its existence?
5. Does modern science agree that the universe began to exist?
6. How would you briefly explain "C." to someone else?

CHAPTER II

$\mathcal{O}$

THE UNIVERSE HAS **ORDER**

For since the creation of the world his invisible attributes,
his eternal power and divine nature, have been clearly seen,
being understood through what has been made, so that they
are without excuse—Romans 1:20

Introduction

Deeply scientific arguments appeal to many modern minds because science is celebrated in the 21st century. Thankfully, Christian apologetics has at its disposal one type of argument for God's existence which makes the case from a scientific and probabilistic perspective. Teleological arguments seek to demonstrate that the complexity of the universe strongly implicates the existence of a designer. The term teleological comes from the Greek word, *telos* which means "ends" or "purpose." What are commonly thought of as design arguments can formally be referred to as teleological arguments because the intent is to show that there is a purpose or end (goal) in the furniture of the universe. As is the case with the cosmological argument, properly articulated teleological arguments are considered to be among the most convincing cases that can be set forth in favor of theism. The late philosopher Anthony Flew, who had been an atheist for most of his career confessed,

> I now believe that the universe was brought into existence
> by an infinite Intelligence. I believe that this universe's

intricate laws manifest what scientists have called the Mind of God. I believe that life and reproduction originate in a divine Source. Why do I believe this, given that I expounded and defended atheism for more than a half century? The short answer is this: this is the world picture, as I see it, that has emerged from modern science.[13]

In what follows, we will examine an example of a formal teleological argument, view objections to the argument, and consider how the argument might best be explained for the average individual. As was the case in chapter one, it will not be appropriate to explain and evaluate all historical versions of design arguments. Instead, we will focus on one example which is in use by modern Christian defenders. If it is the case that the "C." is immediately accessible to the listener because it is based upon premises which are already held by them, then the teleological argument ("O.") is similarly accessible because it is based upon evidence which is immediately visible in the created universe. The universe has ORDER. For this reason, the data which we will consider here is, I believe, digestible to any person of average education. However, before moving forward to consider a formal argument, it is important to say a word about evolutionary biology.

Many ardent defenders of the faith expend a great deal of effort in attempts to debunk the claims of evolutionists. It is true that one will rarely defend a design argument without encountering this subject. Commonly, if the defender himself does not refer to the subject, the listener will. There are mountains of materials produced by intelligent design advocates and creationists which assist believers in dealing with this very important matter. Nevertheless, discussions regarding evolution can often distract listeners from the elegance of a powerful design argument by bogging the presentation down with a secondary concern which is not necessary for the potency of the argument itself.

---

[13] Flew, Anthony, *There is a God: how the world's most notorious atheist changed his mind*, (New York, NY: Harper Collins, 2007), 88.

To be clear, even if evolution were true it would not refute "O." in any way. The reason for this is that an argument from design focuses on more than mere biological life. The complexity and specificity of the created objects of the universe, including the life permitting aspects of it, demand the design conclusion. Such aspects of the created order are somewhat outside the purview of the evolution of biological life on earth. Talking about evolution may result in an interesting discussion, but it does not result in a necessary one for the purpose of this argument.

I realize that this comes as somewhat of a letdown for many readers. Many professional Christian defenders are frustrated by the fact that the evolution debate is the central issue about which outsiders seem to think our discipline focuses. It is not. Likewise, outsiders are often frustrated by the fact that some Christian thinkers refuse to deal with this hotly debated issue. Clearly, this is an interesting and valid area of study for defenders, but it serves to congest and confuse the "O." argument. Especially when evangelism is in view, believers should not involve themselves in secondary issues which will likely do a disservice to the teleological truth they are attempting to explain.

The Formal Argument[14]

One example of a teleological (design) argument is as follows:

1. The fine tuning of the universe is due to either, physical necessity, chance or design.
2. It is not due to physical necessity or chance
3. Therefore, it is due to design.[15]

---

[14] Some citations used in this section are often referenced by William Lane Craig.

[15] Craig, William Lane, *Reasonable Faith*, (Wheaton, IL: Crossway Books; 3 ed. 1998), 161.

The argument is structured in such a way that one must deny the truth of either premise (1) or premise (2) if the conclusion is to be denied. It should be clear how daunting a task this would be to accomplish by the time the argument is explained in detail. Ultimately, the conclusion is, I think, all but inescapable for the thinking individual. It is perhaps for this reason that many classical defenders will incorporate some version of a design argument into their cases for God's existence.

CORE MOMENT

It's simple! The argument just explains that the universe is so incredibly complex either because it just had to be (for some strange reason), it happened by chance (which really seems absurd), or because it was designed by a great designer.

What premise (1) covers are the only three possible explanations for why the universe is so remarkably well ORDERED. There is no debate that the universe is undeniably complex in precisely this way. Atheists and theists alike stand in awe of the magnitude and specificity of the world in which they live. It is humbling and amazing. Such complexity can only be the result of one of three things. First we will consider the possibility of *physical necessity*.

According to this explanation, the universe had absolutely no chance of *not* being life permitting. In other words, the theory of everything (TOE), that theoretical physicists like Stephen Hawking are searching for, will one day be discovered and will explain why the universe could not have existed in any other way. There is simply no reason to think this is the case. It is somewhat like the "naturalism of the gaps" I mentioned in chapter one. Moreover, British physicist P.C.W. Davies writes,

Even if the laws of physics were unique, it doesn't follow that the physical universe itself is unique; the laws of physics must be augmented by cosmic initial conditions; there is nothing in present ideas about "laws of initial conditions" remotely to suggest that their consistency with the laws of physics would imply uniqueness. Far from it, it seems, then, that the physical universe does not have to be the way that it is: it could have been otherwise.[16]

This means that physical necessity will not do as an explanation.

CORE MOMENT

In simpler words, the idea that the universe is so complex because it just had to be that way fails. There is no reason to think the universe couldn't have been a lot of different ways. So there must be a better reason why the universe seems to be finely tuned for life.

Ideas like this are representative of an *a priori* adoption of naturalism. The sentiment is, "no matter how outlandish the hypothesis must be, it must be a naturalistic hypothesis that does not involve God." For obvious reasons this is irrational. If one assumes naturalism from the beginning, then it will always be the case that one will arrive at a naturalistic conclusion. The now famous quote from Richard Lewontin resonates here. He says,

It is not that the methods and institutions of science somehow compel us to accept a material explanation of the phenomenal world, but, on the contrary, that we are forced

---

[16]   Davies, Paul, *The Mind of God*, (New York, NY: Simon & Shuster, 1992), 169.

by our a priori adherence to material causes to create an apparatus of investigation and a set of concepts that produce material explanations, no matter how counter-intuitive, no matter how mystifying to the uninitiated. Moreover, that materialism is an absolute, for we cannot allow a Divine Foot in the door.[17]

It is because of this that some atheists assert a number of strikingly awkward explanations for the data about reality that modern science has unveiled.

Chance does little more to explain the complexity and specificity of the universe. According to this explanation, mere chance led to the ordering of the universe in such a way that it was appropriate for life. Mankind is simply the happy recipient of the blessing of chance. Of all of the innumerable ways the universe could have come to exist, we are just unbelievably lucky that it turned out this way. However, chance will not do as a fitting explanation.

The chances of the universe being life permitting has been estimated by Davies to be one in 10 to the 100th power. This number is so unthinkably high that a smaller number should be considered in order to even provide an adequate analogy. Take for example, the balance necessary between electrons and protons. This alone necessitates an accuracy of one in 10 to the 37th power. Astrophysicist Hugh Ross eloquently describes the chances of this occurring without design thusly,

> One part in 10 to the 37th power is such an incredibly sensitive balance that it is hard to visualize. The following analogy might help: Cover the entire North American continent in dimes all the way up to the moon, a height of about 239,000 miles. (in comparison, the money to pay for

---

[17] Lewontin, Richard, *Billions and Billions of Demons*, (The New York Review, 9 January 1997), 31.

the U.S. federal government debt would cover one square mile less than two feet deep with dimes.) Next, pile dimes from here to the moon on a million other continents the same size as North America. Paint one dime red and mix it into the billion piles of dimes. Blindfold a friend and ask him to pick out one dime. The odds that he will pick the red dime are one in 10 to the 37th power. And this is only one of the parameters that is so delicately balanced to allow life to form.[18]

Clearly, chance cannot explain the complexity and specificity of the universe. Remember, the above quote only refers to one of the necessary parameters. It is simply inconceivable that the universe randomly resulted in a life permitting situation.

CORE MOMENT

This just goes to show that the idea that the universe is so complex and fit for life because of chance is really ridiculous. So there really is only one alternative.

This leaves only one option. Design is the only means by which the universe could have been produced in such a way that it is ordered and life permitting. Critics must either demonstrate that there is some other means by which the universe could have become so well ordered, or except the design hypothesis. The choice should seem clear to thinking people. For these reasons it is sensible to move forward and consider further objections to the design argument.

---

18   Ross, Hugh, *The Creator and the Cosmos*, (Colorado Springs, CO: NavPress Publ. Group, Enlarged 3rd Ed. 2001), 150.

Further Objections

CORE MOMENT

These objections can get kind of technical. If you're a beginner, it might be a good idea to just focus on the actual argument we've covered so far. You can always come back to these objections once you've grown in your understanding a little more. If you think you're ready then keep reading. Just don't get discouraged if it's tough at first.

What if there are numerous other universes?

Such a challenge appeals to the possibility that the universe came to be life permitting by sheer chance. Of this, Ed Harrison writes, "The fine tuning of the universe provides *prima facie* evidence of deistic design. Take your choice: blind chance that requires multitudes of universes, or design that requires only one."[19] Nevertheless, the idea behind this objection is that the more universes exist, the greater the probability that one individual universe would happen to be life permitting. It is referred to technically as a *multiverse* or *universe/ world ensemble*. Prominent biologist and atheist spokesperson, Richard Dawkins, has famously argued for this explanation. Nevertheless, despite Dawkins' rejection of this main criticism, the existence of multiple universes would result in a much more complex situation than currently exists. For this reason, Dawkins postulated a simple mechanism by which these complex universes were created. The *oscillating universe* is described by Dawkins as follows:

---

[19] Harrison, Ed, *Masks of the Universe*, (New York, NY: Collier Books, Macmillan, 1985), 252, 253.

> Our time and space did indeed begin in our big bang, but
> this was just the latest in a long series of big bangs, each
> one initiated by the big crunch that terminated the previous
> universe in the series. Nobody understands what goes on in
> singularities such as the big bang, so it is conceivable that
> the laws and constants are reset to new values, each time. If
> bang-expansion-contraction-crunch cycles have been going
> on forever like a cosmic accordion, we have a serial, rather
> than parallel, version of the multiverse.[20]

The problem with this hypothesis is that cosmologists have strong
reason to believe that if an oscillating model exists, universes would
get larger with each new universe created. This would mean that as
the history of the multiverse is traced backwards, the universes would
become much smaller with each generation. In fact, astronomer, Joseph
Silk, has determined that there can only have been 100 universes or
less if this model is correct.[21] What this means is that the oscillating
model, if true, would produce far too few universes to justify a belief
in order by chance.

It is also worth addressing the resetting of values of which
Dawkins speaks. Even if these values were reset, there must be
underlying values that are constants. They themselves require
explanation. Anthony Flew explains,

> Some have said that the laws of nature are simply accidental
> results of the way the universe cooled after the big bang.
> But . . . even such accidents can be regarded as secondary
> manifestations of deeper laws governing the ensemble of
> universes. Again, even the evolution of the laws of nature

---

[20]   Dawkins, Richard, *The God Delusion*, (New York, NY: Bantam Press,
2008), 174.

[21]   Silk, Joseph, *The Big Bang*, (San Fransisco, CA: Freeman Press, 2nd ed.,
1989), 311, 312.

and changes to the constants follow certain laws. We're still left with the question of how these "deeper" laws originated. No matter how far you push back the properties of the universe as somehow "emergent," their very emergence has to follow certain prior laws. So multiverse or not, we still have to come to terms with the origin of the laws of nature. And the only viable explanation here is the divine Mind.[22]

Though Flew is not specifically referring to an oscillating model, his claims regarding the emergence of new laws is applicable. Something constant determines the laws of new universes, and those constants require an origin themselves.

CORE MOMENT

The atheist is saying that the universe has happened over and over so many times that the chances of a universe being life permitting is more reasonable. The problem is that even if the universe had gone through cycles like this, it couldn't have happened enough times to increase the odds in any serious way.

A second mechanism for the development of numerous universes which is defended by Dawkins is a sort of evolutionary cosmology suggested by Lee Smolin. Dawkins explains it thusly,

Daughter universes are born of parent universes, not in a fully fledged big crunch, but more locally in black holes. Smolin adds a form of heredity: The fundamental

---

[22] Flew, Anthony, *There is a God: how the world's most notorious atheist changed his mind*, (New York, NY: Harper Collins, 2007), 121,122.

constants of a daughter universe are slightly "mutated" versions of the constants of its parent . . . Those universes which have what it takes to "survive" and "reproduce" come to predominate in the multiverse. "What it takes" includes lasting long enough to "reproduce." Because the act of reproduction takes place in black holes, successful universes must have what it takes to make black holes. This ability entails various other properties. For example, the tendency of matter to condense into clouds and then stars is a prerequisite for making black holes. Stars also . . . are the precursors to the development of interesting chemistry, and hence life. So, Smolin suggests, there has been a Darwinian selection of universes in the multiverse, directly favoring the evolution of black hole fecundity and indirectly favoring the production of life.[23]

The difficulty with this claim is that physicists have determined that Smolin's theory is flawed. Stephen Hawking was once hopeful of this sort of mechanism but regretfully admitted, "There is no baby universe branching off, as I once thought."[24]

CORE MOMENT

This time the atheists are saying that universes "give birth" to new universes. Maybe this would result in enough new universes to raise the odds of a life permitting one by chance. Nope. Even one of the most famous atheist thinkers (Hawking) admits that it doesn't work.

---

[23] Dawkins, Richard, *The God Delusion*, (New York, NY: Bantam Press, 2008), 175.

[24] Hawking, Stephen, *Information Loss in Black Holes*, (http://arxiv.org/abs/hep-th/0507171). Internet. Accessed on 10 July, 2012.

For these reasons, the multiverse hypothesis will not do as an adequate defense of chance as the means by which the universe became so well ordered for life. Furthermore, the obvious and apparent reason to reject such a hypothesis is that it is completely *ad hoc*. There is absolutely no evidence to suggest such a universe ensemble. Therefore, we may move forward to consider another objection.

What about the anthropic principle?

Another objection to the design argument is that regardless of how the universe came to be so well ordered for life, the claim by humans that it appears to have been designed is just what we should expect based on the anthropic principle. In other words, if the universe were not life permitting, no one would be here to notice that it is not life permitting. Thus, any universe that is life permitting is, by definition, going to seem well ordered for life.

CORE MOMENT

What atheists want to say here is that the universe only seems well designed to you because you happen to be here. It doesn't sound like much of an argument, does it?

There are a couple of comments that need to be made about this objection. First, this does not actually deal with "O." directly. It is more of a cop-out. Second, the anthropic principle is more of a description of the nature of reality than an evidence against theism. Finally, this sort of an explanation would never be accepted by thinkers in any uncontroversial area.

Guillermo Gonzalez and Jay Wesley Richards describe an analogy of this problematic use of the anthropic principle.

Imagine an American Intelligence officer, captured by the Nazi SS during World War II, who is sentenced to death by a firing squad. Because of this officer's importance, the SS assign fifty of Germany's finest sharpshooters to his execution. After lining him up against a wall, the sharpshooters take their positions three meters away. Upon firing, however, the officer discovers that every single sharpshooter has missed, and that instead, their fifty bullets have made a perfect outline of his body on the wall behind him. What would we think if the officer reflected on his situation, and then responded, "I suppose I shouldn't be surprised to see this. If the sharpshooters hadn't missed, I wouldn't be here to observe it"? We would rightly wonder what he was doing in intelligence, since the more sensible explanation would be that, for some reason, the execution had been rigged. Perhaps the sharpshooters had been ordered to miss, or they had colluded with one another for some unknown reason. In short, the best explanation would be that the event was the product of intelligent design. Shrugging one's shoulders and concluding that it's a chance occurrence is just dense.[25]

What these authors are attempting to get across is that the fact of the anthropic principle does not speak against the truth of theism. Thus, this objection fails as a compelling defense of the claim that the universe is finely-tuned because of chance or physical necessity. With this, we may now move forward to discuss even more objections.

---

[25] Gonzalez, Guillermo & Richards, Jay Wesley, *The Privileged Planet*, (Washington, DC: Regnery Publishing, 2004), 267.

Are there not many highly unlikely things that
happen which are not the result of design?

What this question seeks to demonstrate is that chance could result in a life permitting universe since there are many examples of highly unlikely events that are clearly the result of chance. After all, everything that happens is, in a certain sense, highly unlikely. When one considers the fact that the odds were against the birth of any one person on planet earth, this becomes clear. Of all the random sperm cells and all the random eggs that could have met, you were the happy and highly unlikely result of exactly the sperm and egg that joined. Is not this a highly unlikely yet random event?

A similar example was given by Harvard graduate and Florida International University professor of world religions, Daniel Alvarez, when we debated the evidence for God's existence in 2010. He argued that the winner of a nation-wide lottery might feel as though there must have been some design in his fortunate success. Moreover, there had to be a winner, and even though the chances of any single specific person winning were incredibly low, chance led to their incredibly unlikely good fortune. However, this misses the point in a noteworthy way.

When Christian defenders talk about the fine-tuning of the universe, they are not merely referring to the unlikely complexity of the universe. They are referring to the *specified complexity* of the universe. The difference should be clear. When cards are dealt in a poker game, every possible arrangement of cards is incredibly unlikely. In fact, they are all equally unlikely. Nevertheless, when a player is dealt a royal flush they have received the most powerful hand in the game. This represents specified complexity. Naturally, this has happened by chance. Yet, when the same player receives the royal flush, other players have good reason to be suspicious. If he gets the royal flush more than once in the same game, or even in the same month, they may be justified in questioning his honesty in the game. Perhaps he is cheating. In more specific terms, it looks like his hand was dealt by design. The specified complexity of the universe being life permitting is not just a matter of complexity, like any weak arrangement of cards. Rather, it is like getting a royal flush almost every time you play the game.

In the case of the lottery, everyone involved knows that one thing is certain, someone will win the game. If two adult humans of opposite sexes with healthy reproductive systems attempt to procreate, it is highly likely that they will ultimately succeed in joining some sperm cell with some egg. For this reason, these are poor analogies, and the argument still stands.

What about poorly designed things?

It is not uncommon for atheists to attack the idea of a designer by arguing that there are a number of things in the universe which seem poorly designed. If there truly is a designer then why would he create a universe with so many apparent problems? The claim is that this counts as evidence against the existence of God. The late atheist (or to use his term "anti-theist"), Christopher Hitchens commonly put the objection thusly,

> Of the other bodies in our solar system alone, the rest are either far too cold to support anything recognizable as life, or far too hot. The same, as it happens, is true of our own blue and rounded planetary home, where heat contends with cold to make large tracts of it into useless wasteland, and where we have come to learn that we live, and have always lived, on a climatic knife edge. Meanwhile, the sun is getting ready to explode and devour its dependant planets like some jealous chief or tribal deity. Some design![26]

---

[26] Hitchens, Christopher, *God is Not Great: How Religion Poisons Everything,* (New York, NY: Twelve Hachet Book Group, paperback, 2009), 80.

There are at least two responses that need to be made with respect to such an objection.

Initially, it should be said that alleged examples of bad design are best discussed case by case. For example, issues like the explosion of our sun are not problems for Christian theists, as all Christians believe in some basic eschatological truths which involve the resurrection and glorification of the natural world at the end of time. Moreover, there are a number of claims like this, which when carefully examined, fail because the item which seems poorly designed turns out to be incredibly appropriate for its function.

Second, even if something is poorly designed, it is still *designed*. In 2010 I had the privilege of holding an apologetics conference in Miami, Florida at a church which was overwhelmingly made up of Cuban-Americans. Over lunch we discussed Cuban culture in great detail. One of the interesting facts they shared was the existence of a poorly designed automatic transmission automobile manufactured in Cuba known as a Futingo. Futingos, as best I could gather, have become infamous for their lack of reliability. They are something of a joke to Cubans. Nevertheless, while everyone admits that a Futingo is a poorly designed car, no one denies that the Furingo was actually designed. Thus, while most Christian theists will deny that the designer is a poor one, the existence of what seem to be poorly designed items in the universe is not evidence of a lack of design in the universe.

For all of the reasons listed here, Christian theists should feel confident in the argument that the universe is well ordered. Repeatedly, atheists and agnostics have attempted to demonstrate that the argument fails and have failed in their endeavors. Until some skeptic is able to show and defend either a fourth option (other than physical necessity, chance or design) which explains the fine-tuning of the universe, or is able to successfully articulate a defense of the two existing alternatives to design, the argument that the universe is ORDERED because of design stands undefeated.

Transitioning the Argument for the Layman

The argument explained in this chapter is one with which many church members are already somewhat familiar. Referring to it as "the design argument" is likely to jog their memory more easily than calling it "the teleological argument for God's existence." However, it has received a great deal of coverage via the media over the years and has made its way into sermons in casual form. Still, the only attention paid to it by most laymen comes with respect to the debate regarding evolution. Once again, this is an important discussion that needs to be had, but for the purpose of evangelism learners need to know how to successfully articulate the argument from design well. Learning some bumper-sticker one-liners which cast aspersion on evolution may be satisfying to some evangelicals, but it can be a distraction from the greater truth that is revealed by the argument. Moreover, it confuses the discussion by evoking political conversations about what should be taught in public school science classes. Such dialogues are vital in the right context, but the goal of Christians should be to reach the hearts and minds of unbelievers first, not win a debate.

For this reason, training on the argument should begin by pointing out what is not necessary to make the case. Students do not need to know one single fact about biology to successfully share the case from order with unbelievers. Facilitators can share premise (1) with the students by pointing out that the world became so well ordered for life either, "because it just had to be this way, it randomly ended up this way, or God designed it for life." When students wish to defend premise (1), they merely need to ask the unbeliever whether there are any other options which he can think of to explain the order of the universe. There aren't any. Whatever the unbeliever mentions as a possibility will either be a misunderstanding of the argument or will fall into one of the three categories. For this reason the student can move on to the defense of premise (2). This is where most of the action takes place for this argument.

It should seem intuitively obvious to students that the universe did not, in fact, have to be this way. One could point out the varying citations mentioned in this chapter that demonstrate that scientists today admit that it could have been otherwise. This, however, shouldn't really be necessary. The learners know that when something explodes, it is consistent with explosions for debris to fly in any number of directions. A plate might shatter into any arrangement of glass shards. If an explosion in a lumber yard resulted in a finely constructed log cabin, no one would contend that the explosion just had to result in a move-in ready home. What about chance?

Awareness of the absurdity of chance as an explanation for the fine-tuning of the universe is what laymen already have because of prior learning. Tornados in junk yards do not result in 747 airliners, and they would not result in 747s given billions of tornados in billions of junkyards. Remember, we are not talking about the complexity of biological life, we are talking about the ordering of the entire universe for life. This raises the bar considerably. Unbelievers, with whom students might converse, will point out that in biological evolution there is a mechanism for arriving at complexity via natural selection. This is not the case with the fine-tuning of the universe *for* life. No such mechanism exists. Thus, fine-tuning of this sort must be by a truest sense of chance. This is absurd. A simple analogy like Hugh Ross' "dimes to the moon" example may be memorable enough with which to supply students for their own apologetic uses. It is a powerful explanation. When most common unbelievers say that it all just happened by chance, they usually have no idea of how unthinkably outlandish such a claim is.

At this point the student can move forward to show that the only viable alternative is that the universe is the product of design. If unbelievers wish to push their objections further, they can only claim that some other super-intellect besides God functioned as the designer. Yet, this only pushes the argument back a step. Who designed the super-intellect? Students should be prepared for the ever-present *tu quoque* fallacy, "Who made God?" This objection is covered in chapter one. Truly, a reasonable unbeliever must admit that the evidence leads to the conclusion that God exists.

Conclusion

In this chapter we have covered the "O." argument in a fair amount of detail. The universe is incredibly well ORDERED for life. Learners should be able to digest and present the case from design without much difficulty. Furthermore, if they follow the advice of avoiding the subject of evolution, they do not need to understand complex matters of biology to persuasively present the argument. As is true of the "C." argument, most of the basic ideas at play here are already acceptable to the student and the unbeliever alike. It is not difficult for facilitators and students to creatively formulate their own analogies to support the denial of the two alternatives to design.

The objections brought by skeptics today fail across the board; either because they are out of step with modern science, like Dawkins' mechanisms for the creation of multiple universes, or because they merely serve as red herrings that miss the point like Hitchens' examples of poor design. We are standing at a time in the history of the world in which good science has revealed itself to be quite hospitable to theism.

The "O." argument itself demands that the universe is either the result of physical necessity, chance or design. As explained above, the former two alternatives fail miserably and the latter alternative fits the evidence. There is no reason to believe that the universe simply had to be life permitting. Moreover, the data contained here demonstrates that it did not. It is prohibitively unlikely that the universe came to be so well ORDERED for life by chance alone. On the basis of this argument, the most reasonable thing for a thinking person to do is accept the truth of God's existence.

Questions

1. Why does the "O." in C.O.R.E. F.A.C.T.S. stand for *Ordered*?
2. What are the three possible explanations for the well ordered (finely-tuned) universe?
3. Why is it that chance will not explain the order?
4. Why is it that physical necessity will not explain the order?
5. What is wrong with the idea that some super-intellect besides God may be responsible?
6. Why might it be helpful to avoid the subject of evolution?

CHAPTER III

THE UNIVERSE HAS **RULES**

When the Gentiles who do not have the law do instinctively the things of the law, these, not having the law, are a law to themselves, in that they show the work of the law written in their hearts, their conscience bearing witness—Romans 2:14,15

Introduction

Shockingly, one of the most intrinsically compelling arguments for God's existence is also one that is often discounted by believers and unbelievers alike. The moral argument has undeniably captured the attention of many skeptics and lifted them out of their intellectual doubts and settled them onto firm theistic foundations. Yet, some have considered it to be an elaborate case of question begging. What cannot be denied is its usefulness in convincing skeptics of the truth of Christian theism. Francis Collins, the head of the human genome project, describes his experience of the argument as follows:

> Encountering this argument at age twenty-six, I was stunned by its logic. Here, hiding in my own heart as familiar as anything in daily experience, but now emerging for the first time as a clarifying principle, this Moral law shone its bright white light into the childish recesses of my

atheism, and demanded a serious consideration of its origin. Was this God looking back at me?[27]

Most famously, C.S. Lewis articulated the argument in his classic, *Mere Christianity*. Thus, since the second half of the 20th century, atheist philosophers have been arguing against it and Christian philosophers have been using it. Though it does not rely on the scientific sophistication of the design ("O.") argument, nor the epic grandeur of the cosmological ("C.") argument, it is born out of a reflection upon the human experience and what that experience demonstrates about the nature of reality.

In this chapter, our discussion will focus on a proper articulation of a moral argument in use by Christian philosophers in the 21st century. The "R." stands for RULES because the existence of moral values and duties result in *Rules* for mankind. We will examine objections to the argument as well as consider how the argument might best be explained to, and defended by, the layman. Ultimately, readers will find an argument for God's existence which is immediately accessible to them and is difficult to dismiss.

The Formal Argument

At present, William Lane Craig's moral argument[28] is the most repeated and defended formal articulation of the case. He states his moral argument thusly,

1. If God does not exist, objective moral values and duties do not exist.
2. Objective moral values and duties do exist.

---

[27]   Collins, Francis, *The Language of God*, (New York, NY: Simon & Schuster, 2006), 29.

[28]   Craig, William Lane, *On Guard*, (Paris, Ontario: David C. Cook; New ed., 2010), 129.

3. Therefore, God exists.

For the truth of the argument to sink in, thinkers need to be aware of what is meant by objective and subjective moral values and duties. If something is objectively true, it means that it is true no matter what anyone thinks about it. In other words, it is not a matter of opinion. Mathematics are objective in this way. Two plus two equals four. If it were the case that everyone on planet earth disagreed with this claim, it would still be the case that two plus two does equal four. This is an objective truth. Conversely, subjectivity does deal with matters that are relative. Whether or not chocolate ice cream tastes the best or bald men are the most attractive kinds of men are subjective questions. The answers will depend on one's personal opinions or the consensus of society. Examples are prevalent of the chaos that can ensue when one mistakenly categorizes something as subjective which is actually objective.

Relativism is a fine example of this misstep. Cognitive relativists hold that all truth is relative. What is meant by this is that truth is subjective. For example, it is not only a subjective statement to say that chocolate ice cream is the best flavor, but the cognitive relativist would also claim that the existence of the planet earth is also subjective. That is to say, he would have to hold, if he is going to be consistent in his cognitive relativism, that whether the earth exists is a matter of opinion. This extends to all truth. Situational relativists claim that the truth depends on the circumstances. Moral relativists hold that absolute, or objective, truths do exist, but moral values and duties are not objective in this way. One can see how relativism is dangerous territory precisely because it categorizes certain things as subjective which should be considered objective. It is for this reason that Peter Kreeft warns, "No culture in history has ever embraced moral relativism and survived. Our own culture, therefore, will either (1) be the first, and disprove history's clearest lesson, or (2) persist in its relativism and die, or (3) repent of its relativism and live. There is no other option."[29]

CORE MOMENT

It might help to think of objective things as "factual" and subjective things as "matters of opinion."

Another point of clarification needs to be made with respect to the terms *values* and *duties*. A value is something that is good or bad. Conversely, a duty is something that is right or wrong. Exercise is good, but sickness is bad. However, treating others well is right, while murdering others is wrong. This is the distinction in Craig's argument between moral values and moral duties. From here we can move forward to discuss how the argument works.

The claim of premise (1) is that if God doesn't exist then moral values and duties which are objective, or absolute, do not exist. The reason for this is simply that if God does not exist then it becomes a matter of opinion whether something is truly right or wrong. As Francis Schaeffer rightly explains,

> If there is no absolute moral standard, then one cannot say in a final sense that anything is right or wrong. By absolute we mean that which always applies, that which provides a final or ultimate standard. There must be an absolute if there are to be morals, and there must be an absolute if there are to be real values. If there is no absolute beyond man's ideas, then there is no final appeal to judge between

---

[29] Kreeft, Peter, *The Philosophy of Jesus*, (South Bend, IN: St. Augustine Press, 1st ed. 2007), 118.

individuals and groups whose moral judgments conflict. We
are merely left with conflicting opinions.[30]

What higher authority would we appeal to in making the claim
that it is wrong to murder, rape, steal or treat others unkindly? One's
governmental edicts or laws will not do because they represent the
subjective decisions of a nation or national leaders. That is to say, the
laws in one nation can, and often do, differ from the laws of another
nation. For this reason, when you leave one nation where it is against
the law to buy and sell marijuana and enter another nation where it is
legal to buy and sell marijuana, you discover that the legality of the
buying and selling of marijuana is subjective and dependent on whose
laws are at play. Without God, moral values and duties are subjective.
If God does exist, then moral values and duties are objective.

In a world without God there is no intrinsic purpose to human life.
Strikingly, many atheists have admitted this. It is for this very reason
that existential atheist, Jean Paul Sartre, described man as creating
purpose for himself. He passionately writes,

> But in reality and for the existentialist, there is no love apart
> from the deeds of love; no potentiality of love other than
> that which is manifested in loving; there is no genius other
> than that which is expressed in works of art. The genius of
> Proust is the totality of the works of Proust; the genius of
> Racine is the series of his tragedies, outside of which there
> is nothing. Why should we attribute to Racine the capacity
> to write yet another tragedy when that is precisely what
> he—did not write? In life, a man commits himself, draws
> his own portrait and there is nothing but that portrait . . .
> What we mean to say is that a man is no other than a series

---

[30]   Schaeffer, Francis, *How Should We Then Live*, (Wheaton, IL:Crossway, 50th
Anniversary L'abri ed., 2005), 145.

of undertakings, that he is the sum, the organization, the set of relations that constitute these undertakings.[31]

For Sartre, man is what he does. But this, by no means, requires any real purpose of him. His purpose is subjective and dependent upon what obligations he chooses to accept or assign for himself.

Some naturalists might contend that man does have one simple purpose, namely, the propagation of his own genetic material for the sustaining of his species. While this is descriptive of what biological beings do, it is not something that they must do. That is to say, they are not morally culpable for not doing so. Thus, naturalism can provide no real purpose for the human race. However, it gets worse than that.

Similarly, and flowing from this, in the absence of God there are no moral values or duties. Atheist thinker Frederick Nietzsche recognized this and it was the genesis of his famous, "God is dead" statement. Here, it will simply suffice to say that if there is no God, everything is permissible and nothing has value.

Ultimately, the truth of atheism would mean that we may only properly refer to man as liking kindness and disliking murder. We cannot say that kindness is good or murder is wrong. This strikes most people as horrid, but it is even more deplorable when one considers even more horrendous events in human history. As many Christian defenders have pointed out, the holocaust of the Jews would, if there is no God, not be a bad thing. It would just be a thing. Worse still, there would be no moral difference between humanitarian efforts in Africa and the genocide of the Jews. What these would represent, are just different things that different humans like to do. Only a little better, we could say that they were different things that different humans thought should be considered right. Nevertheless, on atheism they are neither right nor wrong. They just are.

---

[31]   Marino, Gordon, *Basic Writings of Existentialism*, (New York, NY: Random House, 2004), 355, 366.

CORE MOMENT

If it sounds complicated, it's not. It's either your opinion that torturing children, stealing and murdering people are morally wrong or it's a matter of fact that they're wrong. If God doesn't exist, then it's only a matter of opinion. In other words, when you say it's wrong to steal, I can always say, "says who?" The problem is that we all know those things are wrong and that other things are right. We know it as a matter of fact. But if it's a matter of fact, then God exists.

What I am not saying is that we should believe that God exists just because of how awful it would be if morality were subjective. What I am saying is that our certain knowledge that acts like the holocaust are deplorable and acts like building wells in Africa are admirable is clear evidence that morality is objective and that God does exist. This sort of knowledge is wired into humans. It is not wired into the animal kingdom.

When a snake devours a mouse, or a black widow spider cannibalizes her mate, we recognize that the predator devoured its prey, but we would never say that it murdered its prey. Forced copulation occurs with great regularity in the animal kingdom, yet no one charges the male with rape. This is because mankind recognizes that morality is a special aspect of *humanity*, which is not necessarily binding for other earthly beings. All of this serves to confirm the truth of moral objectivity and the existence of God from whom morality springs.

Objections to Premise 1

CORE MOMENT

These objections can get kind of technical. If you're a beginner, it might be a good idea to just focus on the actual argument we've covered so far. You can always come back to these objections once you've grown in your understanding a little more. If you think you're ready then keep reading. Just don't get discouraged if it's tough at first.

Can't culture decide on moral principles that we then consider objective?

This points to an argument that morality can become objective on the basis of what the consensus of a given nation or people group thinks is best. What becomes problematic is that while there will be moral principles which overlap between any two people groups, there will also be moral differences. If the only authority on morality is represented by the consensus, and the consensus differs from one group to the next, then in what way would the morality be objective? J. Budziszewski points out that,

> The whole meaning of morality is a rule that we ought to obey whether we like it or not. If so, then the idea of creating a morality we like better is incoherent. Moreover, it would seem that until we had created our new morality, we would have no standard by which to criticize God. Since we have not yet created one, the standard by which we judge

Him must be the very standard that He gave us. If it is good
enough to judge Him by, then why do we need a new one?[32]

In fact, a better explanation of moral subjectivity would be hard
to locate. Also, we find that for any given nation in the history of the
world, accepted moral principles have undergone change.

Furthermore, most people do not realize what they are saying when
they argue that nations could create objective moral values. What if
extreme Muslim fundamentalists succeeded in overthrowing the
western world's major powers and instituted their view of morality as
law? Suddenly it would become objectively morally right for women
to hide their faces, for all to worship only Allah, and to put infidels to
death. I find it hard to believe that any atheist would find this morally
right. The reason for this is that such a view of morality as is decided
by anyone is not objective but subjective. If it is subjective then it is
not absolute. If it is not absolute, then nothing is really right or wrong,
good or bad. C.S. Lewis clarifies,

> If 'good' or 'better' are terms deriving their sole meaning
> from the ideology of each people, then of course ideologies
> themselves cannot be better or worse than each other.
> Unless the measuring rod is independent of the things
> measured, we can do no measuring, For the same reason it
> is useless to compare the moral ideas of one age with those
> of another: progress and decadence are alike meaningless
> words.[33]

---

[32] Budziszewski, J., *What We Can't Not Know*, (San Francisco, CA: Ignatius
Press, 2003), 12.

[33] Lewis, C.S., *Christian Reflections*, (Grand Rapids, MI: Wm. B. Eerdmans
Publishing, 1995), 73.

CORE MOMENT

If a group of people decide what should be good or bad, right or wrong, then that morality is definitely their opinion (subjective). It doesn't work.

Isn't humanity's shared desire for happiness an objective foundation for morality?

The idea here is that since all men desire happiness, we can locate objective moral values without God by recognizing morality as the principles which lead to human happiness. Still, this objection fails to recognize that humans find happiness in very diverse ways. While one man finds happiness in treating others kindly, some men achieve happiness by committing theft, devouring human flesh, sexually abusing children and ignoring the well-being of others. Even if it were the case that all mankind found happiness in the same activities, simply deciding that this is a foundation for moral values or duties is still subjective. That is to say, it is still just an opinion about what people should do. It would not mean that it is necessarily wrong to break free of the societal opinion and act alternatively.

Isn't humanity's shared desire to flourish an objective foundation for morality?

Differing slightly from the previous objection, this idea recognizes that men find happiness in diverse and conflicting ways. Instead, it refines the notion to an understanding of objective morality based on how humans might best live in harmony. The final response from the last objection still stands. This would still be subjective simply because it represents an opinion about how man should view his own desire for flourishing. Moreover, even if this did demonstrate objective moral values, it does not demonstrate objective moral duties. Just because something is good does not mean man is mandated to do it. From whence does the mandate come? Furthermore, morality based on human flourishing would conflict with man's certain knowledge of what morality is.

If human flourishing is the foundation for moral values then it would lead to a situation in which it would be a moral good to eradicate certain individuals who demonstrate genetically detrimental illnesses and disabilities. Why restrict the flourishing of the world by expending so much effort and money on the treatment of AIDS patients? If the flourishing of our race is the goal, then it would be best to simply euthanize these patients or, at the very least, quarantine them. It is likely the case that many of them will procreate. If they procreate, our collective genes will continue to be corrupted and flourishing will be threatened. Yet, our innate moral values would conflict with such a wicked plan for eradication.

If God is necessary for objective morality, why do atheists often lead moral lives?

This represents a serious misunderstanding of the argument. Christian defenders are not saying that atheists cannot act morally. The fact that they do is evidence of the objectivity of moral values. They too have knowledge of the moral truths that have been hardwired into the human race. This becomes apparent when atheists begin talking about the evils that religion has brought on the human race. Frequently, atheists will argue that the crusades, Spanish inquisition, fundamentalist views on homosexuality and abortion, and misogyny of religious people are all evils that resulted from belief in God. However, their recognition that some of these things are evil is an evidence of their belief in the objectivity of moral values.

If God is necessary for objective morality, why do some believers live amoral lives?

Reversing the problem does not make the point any stronger. That many believers live lives that conflict with morality does not mean that God is not the source of morality. Both atheists and theists can act morally or immorally. This is no better than asking, "If vegetarians believe that eating meat is bad for them, then why do some vegetarians occasionally eat meat?" That vegetarians sometimes eat meat and non-vegetarians sometimes eat salad does not speak to whether or not it is true that eating meat is a bad thing. This is simply a red herring.

Objections to Premise 2

How do we know that morality is objective?

First, one must recognize what this question entails. If morality is not objective then it is necessarily the case that the rape and murder of children is not actually wrong. All we can say, philosophically speaking, is that we don't generally like it. The same is true for any evil thing one can imagine. Conversely, nothing is really right or good. Kindness, mercy and philanthropy are just things that certain people like. It should be clear to any thinking person that this is simply not the way things are.

Second, it is hard to imagine a successful argument for the subjectivity of moral values. In order for an argument to be a good one, the premises of the argument need to be plausible. There is simply no argument in favor of the subjectivity of moral values which contains premises which are more likely to be true than our own immediate and certain knowledge that morality is objective. This may sound like a cop-out, but it is not.

Imagine a similar case. An individual's knowledge of his own existence is a strikingly powerful certainty for him. He *(person A)* may not be able to present external evidence of this truth, but he simply knows that he exists. Now imagine another individual (*person B*) presenting him with an argument that seeks to demonstrate that *person A* does not exist. Perhaps *person B* is able to present powerful data and evidence which counts against *person A's* existence. *Person B* shows *person A* that there is no record of his birth and that there are a number of others who also do not believe that *Person A* exists. *Person B* also provides an elaborate explanation of how *person A* came to believe that he actually exists when, in fact, he does not. Will *person A* accept the claim that he, himself, does not exist? It is very doubtful that he will. The reason for this is simple. No matter how compelling the evidence is that *person A* does not exist, the immediate and certain knowledge *person A* has of his own existence is more plausible than any premise of any imaginable argument *person B* might bring.

Now consider morality. The immediate and certain knowledge that it is wrong to rape and torture children is more powerful and plausible than any premise brought by one who claims that morality is not objective. This may amount to a conversation stopper, but it is what every thinking human, deep down, knows to be true.

Doesn't societal evolution explain why people believe morality is objective?

On this view, morality is just the current result of what is best for the herd. As the idea goes, throughout the evolutionary process our ancestors began to function in a way that would foster survival. It turned out that divisive elements in a group, like what we now call theft and murder, led to a societal implosion with negative effects for every individual in the group. These negative effects naturally extended to the perpetrator of the divisive act as well. Thus, a norm developed within the group which shunned such activities. As this sort of thing continued and became more refined, the negative feelings attached to the self destructive tendencies became more entrenched in the cognitive processes of the mind. Likewise, that which was good for the group, such as an interest in mutual progress, also became a part of the human psyche. Ultimately, the values and duties that humans express today are, therefore, a result of the evolutionary process in a certain sense. What was good for the herd is what we call morality.

This is an attempt to ground human morality in the realm of science. In 2010, Sam Harris released a bestselling work entitled, *The Moral Landscape*, in which he argued that morality is not necessarily subjective on the level of one's favorite flavor of ice cream, but that it really isn't entirely different either. Both can be explained and gauged scientifically. In the afterward of the book he responded to critics who claimed that evaluating morality scientifically merely resulted in a sophisticated yet still subjective framework. Harris provided the argument of his critics and his response by analogy:

It seems to me that there are three, distinct challenges to my thesis put forward thus far:

1. There is no scientific basis to say that we should value well-being, our own or anyone else's. (The Value Problem)
2. Hence, if someone does not care about well-being, or cares only about his own and not about the well-being of others, there is no way to argue that he is wrong from the point of view of science. (The Persuasion Problem)
3. Even if we did agree to grant well-being primacy in any discussion of morality, it is difficult or impossible to define it with rigor. It is, therefore, impossible to measure well-being scientifically. Thus, there can be no science of morality. (The Measurement Problem)

I believe all of these challenges are the product of philosophical confusion. The simplest way to see this is by analogy to medicine and the mysterious quantity we call "health." Let's swap "morality" for "medicine" and "well-being" for "health" and see how things look.

1. There is no scientific basis to say that we should value health, our own or anyone else's. (The Value Problem)

2. Hence, if someone does not care about health, or cares only about his own and not about the health of others, there is no way to argue that he is wrong from the point of view of science. (The Persuasion Problem)

3. Even if we did agree to grant health primacy in any discussion of medicine, it is difficult or impossible to define it with rigor. It is, therefore, impossible to measure health scientifically. Thus, there can be no science of medicine. (The Measurement Problem)

While the analogy may not be perfect, I maintain that it is good enough to nullify these three criticisms.[34]

Clearly, Harris thinks that he has escaped the problem by demonstrating that no one questions the importance of the science of medicine or its focus on human physical health. However, there are two points that need to be made in response. First, health is the self-stated goal of medical practitioners. It is not clear that well-being is the greatest goal in discussions of morality. Harris must assume that it is *a priori* in order for his argument to get off the ground. Second, despite Harris' intent, even his own parallel of the criticisms does not escape the problems shown by them. It *is* the case that "There is no scientific basis to say that we should value health, our own or anyone else's." and that, ". . . if someone does not care about health, or cares only about his own and not about the health of others, there is no way to argue that he is wrong from the point of view of science." Thus, instead of rebutting the criticisms of his adversaries, Harris has only served to make their point again for them.

A major problem with the idea that our morality is based on evolution is also that this would not explain the incredibly selfless

---

34   Harris, Sam, *The Moral Landscape*, (New York, NY: Free Press, 2010), 198-199.

acts that some people display. While it might explain why a mother would jump in front of a car to save her genetic material (her son), it would not explain why an individual would do this for others. Attempts have been made to circumvent such a rebuttal, but in the end, the willingness to give one's own life counts against morality as an evolutionary adaptation.

One final response is important for understanding the moral argument in a robust way. The objectivity of morality is a different subject from the discovery of objective morality. Just as humanity progressively discovers objective mathematical truths, humanity has continued to refine its understanding of objective moral truth. This does not mean that the objective moral truths change. The mathematical principles were always present and true as man refined his understanding of them. While I reject the idea that morality is the result of societal evolution, even if it were the case, it would only speak to how man discovered moral truths. It would not mean that man invented them.

CORE MOMENT

Here the atheist suggests that we evolved our morality. First, that doesn't work. Second, it doesn't matter how we learned what is right and wrong, good or bad. What matters is whether or not those things are factual (not matters of opinion).

What about the Euthyphro dilemma?

In Plato's *Euthyphro*, Socrates asks the character for whom the dialogue is named, whether something is good because it is loved by the gods, or if it is loved by the gods because it is good. Modern atheistic philosophers have pointed to this problem in an attempt to show one of two things. If the good is good because God loves it, then we have a form of voluntarism. This means that God decided on his own moral framework. Yet, this is problematic because most theists (at least Christian theists) view God as *being* good, not just arbitrarily deciding on goodness. Conversely, if God loves the good because it is good then there must exist some higher authority to whom God himself must conform. For obvious reasons this debate has continued since the time of Plato.

There is, however, a third option. If the good flows from God's very nature, then he neither arbitrarily commanded it or recognized it as an external phenomenon. It springs forth from the very being of God. This resolves the dilemma and makes for a view of morality that is truly objective. Hence, both premises of the argument still stand.

Transitioning the Argument for the Layman

With training in view, "R." is revealed to be a somewhat simple apologetic to learn, though mastering it may require more extensive effort. Like "C.," and "O.," the "R." argument is rooted in facts about the nature of reality that should seem clear to students. They need not do extravagant research or spend hours in a library to discover that some things are inherently good and others inherently bad. The existence of right and wrong, likewise, needs no defense. The connecting of dots is really all that a careful facilitator needs to accomplish. What follows is an explanation of the argument that should be easily adopted by learners and retains the powerful philosophical truths it reveals.

It may not seem altogether obvious to students why objective morality cannot exist in the absence of God. What is more, terms like "objective" and "subjective" may represent a foreign language to some individuals. This leads to the practical advice of just removing philosophical terminology from the discussion. Arguments like this one do not need to be stated in this way all of the time. So what does "R." look like in common parlance?

The argument could be set up by asking the following question: "Do you agree that some things are really right and other things are really wrong?" The word "really" is where we would place the term "objectively" in a more formal discussion. Second, one might ask, "Would you also agree that some things are really good and other things are really bad?" At this point it is simple to express the difference between moral values and moral duties. Once they agree, the facilitator can show that certain things are matters of opinion, while other things are matters of fact. It is a fact that $2 + 2 = 4$. It is a matter of opinion whether chocolate or vanilla ice cream is better. The point that the facilitator wants to lead students toward is the truth that moral values and duties are matters of fact in the same way $2 + 2 = 4$ is a fact.

Next, the facilitator can begin discussing premise (1). He can demonstrate that if God does not exist, then real moral values and duties do not exist by pointing out that if God does not exist then there is no authority to which we can appeal when claiming that certain things are right and others are wrong. This may require some discussion, but after the listeners understand why the existence of real moral values and duties implies the existence of God, the conversation can turn to the defense of premise (2).

For beginners, it is helpful to explain what it would mean if there were no real morality. The facilitator should point out that it would mean that things like murder, rape, theft, abuse, genocide, drug use and alcoholism are not really wrong in the same way that $2 + 2 = 7$ is wrong. Undoubtedly, comments like this will get an emotional reaction out of the students. Emotional reactions are not the reason we accept the existence of real morality, but they do show that we all know it exists. As many apologists have asserted, there is no moral difference between Adolf Hitler and Mother Teresa if morality is not real (objective). Before long, it will become abundantly clear to the listeners that opinion-based (subjective) morality is worthless.

A few points of clarification may need to be made by the teacher, but there is not much more necessary for learners to begin practicing the moral argument with each other. All they need to do is make these simple points clear to others. No matter what an unbeliever may say in response to premise (1), the student can simply show that any morality is just opinion-based if God does not exist. In defense of premise (2), they need only point to the skeptic's own certain and immediate knowledge that morality is real in the objective sense. If the skeptic does not accept this, the learner can just ask questions like, "Don't you believe that the rape and murder of little children is wrong? Is it just your opinion that it's wrong?" Naturally, the average person will answer "yes" to the former question and "no" to the latter.

Conclusion

As this chapter demonstrates, it is truly within the realm of possibility for a wide demographic to understand and use a simple version of the "R." argument. Facilitators should be prepared to answer questions on the basis of what is discussed in the totality of this chapter, but the basic principles of the case can be digested without much trouble. Objections to the moral argument can usually be dismissed without much difficulty if the apologist has a careful eye. The majority of the objections fall into a handful of simple categories. They either misunderstand the argument, misunderstand objectivity, fail to understand that God is the only possible source of objective morality, or refuse to admit that morality is objective. The argument itself is quite simple. Without God, there is simply no way to defend the existence of real objective moral values and duties. Yet, the existence of true morality of this sort is evident to any honest, self-reflecting person. Thus, God's existence should be accepted since there are RULES for the human race.

Questions

1. Why does the "R." in C.O.R.E. F.A.C.T.S. stand for *Rules*?
2. What is the difference between objective and subjective things?
3. What does it mean to say that moral values and duties are objectively true?
4. Why is it that God is the only explanation for objective morality?
5. Why is it that mankind can't make up their own objective morality?
6. What is different about humans and animals when it comes to morality?

CHAPTER IV

E

PEOPLE CAN HAVE AN IMMEDIATE EXPERIENCE OF GOD

Ask, and it will be given to you; seek, and you will find; knock, and it will be opened to you—Matthew 7:7

Introduction

While the previous three chapters represent arguments for God's existence, what will be discussed here is more of an invitation to realize and accept the united implication these arguments make. That is to say, if God exists as I believe these arguments demonstrate that he does, then this means something incredibly relevant for the citizens of the world. Ultimately, it means that it is not out of the question that we may have an immediate and personal EXPERIENCE of God. Such an experience further testifies to, and, for the individual who experiences him, makes certain his existence. Clearly, this sort of knowledge of God is a part of one's own personal, subjective, conscious experience, and not available as a proof to unbelievers of the world. However, anyone open to the possibility that God exists can intimately know him by allowing him to speak to their heart as countless others have through the ages.

CORE MOMENT

This one is easy! We'll talk about some interesting and important things, but "E." is just about an invitation to experience God right now as countless other people have. This is especially important as we prepare to begin looking at Jesus in the next chapter.

The Prevalence of Theistic Experience

Throughout the history of the world the vast majority of humanity has believed in the existence of a god or gods. One is hard pressed to ever locate a community of people who do not have some sort of monotheistic or polytheistic belief. What makes this more interesting is that even in those tribes and cultures wherein polytheistic beliefs are prevalent, closer investigation almost always reveals that they too are actually monotheistic in a certain sense. While they do believe in a multitude of supernatural beings that we might refer to as "gods," they also maintain a belief that there is one ultimate creator who was the genesis of even those lesser "gods." This is noteworthy because it shows that the vast majority of the human race has held to the truth that there is one creator who is the rightful object of our worship. Moreover, people in every culture claim to have had experiences with him.

CORE MOMENT

The material here is a little different. Instead of an unbeatable argument for God's existence, I'm talking about these claims of experiences of God just to show that it is not unreasonable to remain open to such an experience. If the vast majority of the people of the world throughout history think they have experienced God, then it seems silly not to remain open-minded to such an experience.

Narrowing our gaze even further, it is common for atheists to point out that even among the most dominant monotheistic religions of the world, there is such a great difference of belief that no one can be expected to believe any of them. After all, Christians, Jews and Muslims believe in very different creators. While I actually agree with this in the most important sense (as a Christian I do not believe the god described by Islam exists, and I don't believe that the God of the Jews can be reached without Jesus), I do find it interesting that all three of these religions claim that the God of Abraham is the one true God. Christianity affirms the totality of the Old Testament, and Islam (false as it is) is purported to be the answer to the Judeo-Christian story. Thus, the three dominant monotheistic religions in the history of the world all claim that the God of the Old Testament exists.

Naturally, one may be skeptical as to whether anyone has ever actually made contact with this seemingly illusive being, but they are in the minority. I admit that the majority has been wrong in the past about a great many things, yet having already discussed three powerful arguments for God's existence, it seems likely to me that many of these experiences are valid. Anyone who questions them in light of the arguments presented in this book, may be engaging in exasperated skepticism. Considering the situation by comparison may help.

Some apologists have framed this evidence with an analogy. If 99 people in a village claim to have met a particular man (*person Q*), and only one individual (*person S*) claims that *person Q* does not exist, which is the more likely to be true? Should we believe that 99 villagers are wrong about the existence of *person Q*, or is it more reasonable to assume that *person S* is mistaken? *Person S* might demand that *person Q* does not exist because he has never seen him, heard his voice or met him at all. However, no thinking person would accept that *person S* is correct about *person Q* on the basis of this evidence. If 99 people claimed to have met *person Q*, and could tell powerful stories of experiences they'd had with him, then it stands to reason that *person S* is merely overly skeptical.

Differences in Experience

Furthermore, of all the multitudes of people throughout human history who believed they had experienced God, if only one of them was correct, then he does exist. The same can be said of those who feel they have personally come to know Jesus Christ. Conversely, it is not true that if only one of them is wrong then God does not exist. A similar analogy can make this point clearer. Instead of a village, lets consider the island of Nassau in the Bahamas.

Imagine a situation wherein many people claimed that Nassau did not exist. However, there were millions of people who claimed to have set foot on Nassau, but were mistaken. Maybe they had indeed been to other islands that they mistook for Nassau. One man, though, had indeed been to the actual island of Nassau, and declared it to the world. He would be among the throngs who claimed to have walked the beaches of the place, but as long as he is indeed correct, then Nassau's existence is sure. Even if all other Nassau believers were wrong, his presence there would mean it was certain.

It has become popular among atheists to point out that Christians are also atheists when it comes to the thousands of other gods of other religions in the world. They say that the only difference between a Christian and a genuine atheist is that the atheist believes in one less God than the Christian does. Statements like this may make great bumper-sticker sermons for atheists, but they represent an argument that is truly flawed. The point that the atheist is trying to make is that there are so many religions in the world making conflicting claims about the creator that they must all be false. Yet, surely this does not follow. Just because there are many false religions does not mean that there is not a single valid one. As with the case of Nassau, there may be many individuals who genuinely but incorrectly believe they have been to the island, but we would never say that, therefore, no one has ever been to Nassau. Instead, it is likely that if there are billions of people who claim to have experienced God but are incorrect in how they describe him, then he does exist. Some of them are just misinterpreting their experiences of him. This is consistent with Christian belief, to say the least.

As Christians we maintain that God reveals himself to all genuine seekers of truth. Thus, it is reasonable to assume that many Christians and non-Christians have had real experiences of the one true God. The problem, as a Christian understands, is that many non-Christians are misled by the existing religions of their own cultures and human sin. Nevertheless, the testimony of the world is that God exists.

I want to issue a challenge to readers at this juncture. As we continue through the material in the subsequent chapters, open your mind up to the God whose existence has been demonstrated thus far. Ask him to make the remaining F.A.C.T.S. clear and digestible for you. Struggle to remain open to his response. Genuine seekers have often reported that God has met this earnest endeavor with affirmation.

Objections

> **CORE MOMENT**
>
> These objections can get kind of technical. If you're a beginner, it might be a good idea to just focus on the actual evidence we've covered so far. You can always come back to these objections once you've grown in your understanding a little more. If you think you're ready then keep reading. Just don't get discouraged if it's tough at first.

Doesn't this just amount to taking it on faith without evidence?

What some skeptics want to say about a point like this is that when believers bring up their own personal experiences they are just appealing to faith, and there is no way that one can know for sure whether another person's own experience is real or not. First, this is why I pointed out at the beginning of this chapter that "E." does not amount to an argument or proof for God's existence. The previous three chapters accomplish that objective. Rather, "E." is an invitation to seekers of truth to have an immediate and personal *experience* of God themselves.

Second, while I am forthright that this does not amount to an argument for God's existence, this chapter does provide a piece of data that requires explanation. The majority of human beings claim to have had experiences of God. This may not be an argument in any formal sense, but it certainly counts as evidence.

What about the ad populum fallacy?

The *ad populum* fallacy states that appealing to what the majority of people believe as a way of establishing truth is inadequate. After all, at one time the majority of people thought that the earth was the center of the universe with the sun in orbit around it. The majority of people were clearly wrong. When someone points out the multitude of religious experiences, atheists will often demand that that person has committed this fallacy. However, this is not what we have done.

First, I have been clear that "E." is not an argument but an invitation instead. Second, I am not claiming that the multitudes of individuals who claim to have had experiences with God proves that God exists. I am presenting this fact about the world as a piece of data that requires explanation. The atheist will answer it in one way, and the believer will answer it in a very different way. The question is, "Which is the more plausible explanation?" I think that of the two options—that they are all mistaken, or they are genuinely interacting with something objective—the second is more plausible.

Transitioning the Presentation for the Layman

What facilitators and trainers need to accomplish for students with "E." is merely that after hearing the arguments from "C.," "O.," and "R.," unbelievers should be encouraged to be open minded to an experience of God in their own lives. Not much time needs to be spent on this point. The supplemental material that comprises most of this chapter is provided only to help skeptics see that there is nothing unreasonable or superstitious in doing this. Of the utmost importance is the clear invitation from the believer to engage this God in a fair and open-minded way.

If a trainer does see the benefit of conveying the data regarding individuals who claim to have experienced God throughout history and geography, he may proceed in the following way. He might ask students to try and name a people-group or culture which began as an atheistic society. He might ask them to name a geographical location in which the belief in God has never been found. Once it becomes clear that these questions receive only negative answers, he is in a position to then ask, "Is it unreasonable then to remain open to the possibility that people have actually had genuine experiences of God?" Once he has illustrated this point to the class he can encourage them to use the same method with particularly difficult skeptics. The primary statement that believers should be instructed to make is, "You can have an immediate EXPERIENCE of God by genuinely seeking him with an open mind today." This will set them up for the remainder of the material to be discussed. Namely, they will be prepared for the evidence in favor of the resurrection of Jesus.

Conclusion

In this chapter I have invited individuals to be open-minded enough to have an immediate experience of God. It has been made clear that this is not really an argument. This is a personal appeal. However, we have considered how trainers and facilitators might best express this point to learners. We also contemplated the fact that individuals claiming to have experienced God is a norm for the human race. Therefore, there is nothing uncommon or out of step with the times about being open-minded in this regard. Ultimately, the most important message of this chapter is that you can have an immediate EXPERIENCE of God by genuinely seeking him with an open mind today.

Questions

1. Why does the "E." in C.O.R.E. F.A.C.T.S. stand for *Experience*?
2. What have most cultures traditionally believed about the existence of God?
3. Based on the "person Q and person S" analogy, what is the reasonable conclusion?

4. What is the author inviting unbelieving readers to do in this chapter?

5. What does the author say is the difference between this chapter and the others?

6. What should believers take away from this chapter?

CHAPTER V

𝓕

THE CRUCIFIXION OF JESUS WAS **FATAL**

And Jesus, crying out with a loud voice, said, "Father, into your hands I commit my Spirit." Having said this, he breathed his last.—Luke 23:46

Introduction

In this chapter, we will begin taking a look at the F.A.C.T.S. of the resurrection of Jesus. Surprisingly, when skeptics seek to discredit the central miracle of the New Testament, they seldom begin in the most obvious place. Rather than scrutinizing his appearances or the testimony of the early church, they often begin by questioning whether Jesus actually died when he was crucified. The argument is like this: (1) Jesus had to die in order to rise from the dead; (2) He never really died; so (3) there was no resurrection. The idea is known as the swoon (or apparent death) theory. After all that Jesus endured leading up to the crucifixion and the hours spent hanging on the tree, some claim that Jesus merely "swooned" on the cross. That is to say, he didn't really die. He simply feigned death or perhaps lost consciousness from blood loss. The soldiers thought he was dead, as did the Jews, but his disciples later revived him and then after a short time he began to reveal himself to others, giving the appearance of resurrection.

CORE MOMENT

Believe it or not, all we are trying to do here is show that Jesus died by Roman crucifixion. It's that simple. We just need to demonstrate this so that later we can show that he really did rise from the dead.

An Old Theory is Making a Come Back

This sort of thinking is experiencing a renaissance. While it was once a common claim made by atheist and agnostic scholars, it is actually resurfacing in an unexpected place. With the continued rise of Islam, including Islamic apologetics, the tools abandoned by most atheists are now being adopted by Muslims. Because the Quran, in Surah 4:157-158, demands, "He did not die, They did not crucify him . . ." Muslims have developed a variety of theories as to what happened at the cross. Most take the words of the Quran to mean that rather than surviving the crucifixion, Jesus was not even the one nailed to the tree. Instead God made it appear as though he was crucified. Some actually maintain that Judas Iscariot was transformed by God to have the appearance of Jesus so that he was mistakenly killed and Jesus escaped. A few Muslim apologists have simply argued the old swoon theory in the same tradition of atheist scholars. This was the position Shabir Ally took in a 2009 debate on the question, "Did Jesus Rise from the Dead?"[35]

The simple problem for this is that to say the evidence for it is weak is to put the matter far too mildly. Islam, including its primary document of faith, did not originate until roughly six hundred years after the events of Jesus' life and ministry. To give it preeminence

---

[35] Craig, William Lane & Ally, Shabir, "Did Jesus Rise from the Dead?," (http://www.brianauten.com/Apologetics/Craig-Ally-Debate2.mp3), Internet. Accessed on 19 July, 2012.

over primary texts from the first century is absurd. If the claims of most Muslims are true, that God made it appear as though Jesus was crucified when in fact he was not, then God is a great deceiver. Moreover, there are a number of items that point to the fatal nature of the crucifixion.

The Evidence

First, it must be understood that there is little question among the majority of scholars that Jesus in fact died by Roman crucifixion. Consider the Roman soldiers who carried out the sentence. These men were professional killers. Making an art out of ending lives, they were so brutal in their executions that the thought of a man surviving is absurd. Added to the crucifixion was the scourging. It was a horrendous ordeal that ended with the subject dramatically injured and fast on his way to death. Clearly, a man could not survive after the scourging for very long. If Jesus had been released after this bloody mess, he still would not have lived. Furthermore, when you remember that this was only the beginning, it becomes obvious how brutal the experience was. Next came the crucifixion itself.

It is hard to imagine any man living through such a thing, particularly without the medical help that we have in the modern world. The claim that the soldiers failed in their attempt to end the life of Jesus will not stick. The Roman legions would roar with laughter at hearing such a suggestion. Eminent New Testament scholar, N.T. Wright explains,

> The hoary old theory that Jesus did not really die on the cross, but revived in the cool of the tomb, has likewise nothing to recommend it, and it is noticeably important that even those historians who are passionately committed to denying the resurrection do not go by this route. Roman soldiers, after all, were rather good at killing people, and

when given a rebel leader to practice on they would have had several motives for making sure the job was done properly . . . I regard this conclusion [that Jesus died] as coming in the same sort of category of historical probability so high as to be visually certain, as the death of Augustus in AD 14 or the fall of Jerusalem in AD 70.[36]

As already mentioned, a Roman executioner was familiar with death. It would be an insult to say of him that he was mistaken about Jesus' fatality. For reasons such as this, German atheist New Testament scholar, Gerd Ludemann, writes, "Jesus' death as a consequence of crucifixion is indisputable."[37] However, if this were the end of the story we would not be compelled to accept Christianity.

CORE MOMENT

We know that Jesus really did die because the scourging alone would have killed him. Roman soldiers were expert killers and it would likely be impossible to survive a crucifixion, even with modern medicine. Historians universally agree that Jesus was crucified by the Romans.

That Jesus died is important to establish, however, so that the resurrection case can get off of the ground. Once the case is made that the crucifixion was fatal for Jesus, it makes the appearances defended in the next chapter much more interesting. How could it be that a man who was dead, was then seen alive by others in various locations and by multitudes of people? Thus, the "F." in F.A.C.T.S. is a vital piece of the case.

---

36   Wright, N.T., *The Resurrection of the Son of God*, (Minneapolis, MN: Fortress Press, 2003), 709, 710.

37   Ludemann, Gerd. *The Resurrection of Christ*, (Amherst, NY: Prometheus, 2009), 50.

Objections

CORE MOMENT

These objections can get kind of technical. If you're a beginner, it might be a good idea to just focus on the actual evidence we've covered so far. You can always come back to these objections once you've grown in your understanding a little more. If you think you're ready then keep reading. Just don't get discouraged if it's tough at first.

How do we know that a New Testament author didn't fabricate the crucifixion?

This objection is somewhat moot since the majority of scholars will grant that Jesus did, in fact, die by crucifixion. However, something should be said as to why this is taken to be historically true. We have multiple independent attestation for the death of Jesus. That is to say, several authors refer to it in separate writings. The story of the crucifixion appears in all four of the gospel accounts and is referred to in the letters of Paul. That this is recorded by various authors lends credibility to the case. However, if one wishes to lay eyes on evidence from outside of the Bible, it is ample.

The greatest historian of ancient Rome, Cornelius Tacitus, records,

> But not all the relief that could come from man, not all the bounties that the prince could bestow, nor all the atonements which could be presented to the gods, availed to relieve Nero from the infamy of being believed to have ordered the conflagration, the fire of Rome. Hence to suppress the rumor, he falsely charged with the guilt, and

punished with the most exquisite tortures, the persons commonly called Christians, who were hated for their enormities. Christus, the founder of the name, was put to death by Pontius Pilate, procurator of Judea in the reign of Tiberius: but the pernicious superstition, repressed for a time, broke out again, not only through Judea, where the mischief originated, but through the city of Rome also.[38]

This refers to the death of Jesus explicitly and may indirectly refer to his resurrection in that it seems to be the only way of understanding the phrase, "pernicious superstition." Yet, the testimonies from ancient literature abound. Lucian of Samosata explains, "The Christians, you know, worship a man to this day—the distinguished personage who introduced their novel rites, and was crucified on that account."[39] Finally, Mara Bar-Serapion asks,

What advantage did the Athenians gain from putting Socrates to death? Famine and plague came upon them as a judgment for their crime. What advantage did the men of Samos gain from burning Pythagoras? In a moment their land was covered with sand. What advantage did the Jews gain from executing their wise King? It was just after that that their kingdom was abolished.[40]

Therefore, we have considerable data from Christians and non-Christians, and from within and outside of the Bible that testify to Jesus' death.

---

[38] Hutchins, Robert Maynard, *Great Books of the Western World: Vol. 15, The Annals and the Histories*, (Chicago, IL: Benton, 1952), XV, 44.

[39] Fowler, H. W. & Fowler, F. G., *The Works of Lucian of Samosata: Death of Pelegrine*, (Oxford, UK: Clarendon, 1949), 11-13.

[40] Bruce, F.F., *The New Testament Documents: Are They Reliable?*, (Downers Grove, IL: InterVarsity Press, 1964), 114.

Aren't Christians just too biased about this?

As there are not many serious objections to the claim that Jesus' wounds at the cross were FATAL, let us focus on a more general objection. Since this chapter is the first of those related to the resurrection of Jesus, it is appropriate to now consider the allegation that Christians have difficulty being objective about the resurrection because of personal bias. This issue is one that the Christian carries so close to his chest that it is reasonable to assume that he cannot honestly assess the facts. We must consider our own motives. Are we merely captives of our own biases? Is it possible that we are driven by our own dreams of an afterlife just so that we can have some sense of peace during this one? Reasonable thinkers must admit that bias is a live factor. Mike Licona, in discussing the Christian conclusion he drew from his research admitted, "I experienced a return to my default position of belief. Still, although I am aware that I cannot overcome my personal bias, I maintain that I can be adequately objective and that my present research is, to the best of my knowledge, an honest investigation of the data."[41] As Licona frankly explains, no scholar can completely eradicate his biases when considering any serious subject, but he can work to limit them. So let us now consider the Christian bias.

The Freudian idea that religious beliefs are the product of wish-fulfillment is a charge that may stick to some faiths, but it will not work with Christianity. The idea is that we cannot suffer through this life without some hope that there is more to come. Indeed, this would be horrible. It would lead to the nihilism that we find in the writings of Nietzsche. He is often credited with gallantly claiming a victory for existential atheism, but this is a misconception. Nietzsche, upon arriving at atheism, was horrified by the way it rendered life

---

[41]   Licona, Mike, *The Resurrection of Jesus: A New Historiographical Approach,* (Downers Grove, IL: Intervarsity Press, 2010), 131.

meaningless. Regarding the passage wherein the claim of God's death is made, one author points out,

> The first thing to notice about this passage is that it is not directed at religious believers but at atheists. It is the atheists who mock the God who isn't there, and it is the atheists that Nietzsche's prophet considers to be the real fools. They are fools because they have not come to terms with the meaning of the death of God. They think that they can get rid of God and immortality but hold on to Christian values and Christian morality.[42]

For Nietzsche, this meant that there was no hope for overcoming the reality and imminence of the grave.

Clearly, it would be horrible to live in a world, Nietzsche's world, without the possibility of everlasting life, but the fact that everlasting life is a wonderful idea does not mean it is not also a fact of reality. This is the first major problem with the charge that Christianity is simply wish fulfillment. It assumes that just because we would like it to be so, it must not be so. Where is the logic in this? There are many things throughout our lives that we hope will happen that actually do happen. Girls dream of the wonder of their wedding day and the day comes. Men dream of becoming wealthy and they become wealthy. It makes no sense to say that Christianity is false and there is no afterlife simply because we would like it to be the truth. Problems persist, however, for the wish-fulfillment case against Christianity.

If our faith merely developed out of a desire to have our wishes fulfilled, then heaven makes perfect sense. One would expect a fabricated afterlife to be rather heavenly. On the other hand, the wish fulfillment hypothesis makes no sense of the Christian teaching regarding the reality of hell. How would we be comforted by the

---

[42]   D'Souza, Dinesh, *Life after Death,* (New York, NY: Regnery Press, 2009), 205,206.

possibility that one day we would pass through a doorway into a world of suffering that is everlasting? For this reason, our desires cannot be credited with the creation of the afterlife. Moreover, it would also fail to explain the moral guidelines that we are meant to live by as Christians in this world. If I am running on wish fulfillment, why would I not create a faith that allowed me to indulge in every pleasure of present earthly existence and then have the promise of heaven on top of that? Wish fulfillment simply does not explain the Christian teachings on hell and obedience.

CORE MOMENT

If Christians just made up their religion then why did they include the possibility of hell and all the talk of obedience? If early Christians just made it up it would seem that they would have made all things permissible.

This is already enough reason to doubt the claim that Christians just dreamed it all up, but there is one more issue to consider. Such an idea ignores the evidence we are offering for the truth claims that we make. We are not saying that Christianity is true because we hope that it is. We are saying that there is good reason to believe that what Jesus taught was factual. The argument that this is simply wish fulfillment just ignores the evidence. I would not want to be in the same boat with Nietzsche, but if he was right and atheism was true, I would be forced to join him in God's funeral dirge. Thankfully, he was wrong. I believe in Christian theism not because I would like it to be true; there are things as a human I wish were different, but I believe because they *are* true.

Transitioning the Presentation for the Layman

The "F." stands for "FATAL," because Jesus' wounds at the crucifixion were fatal. The first point that needs to be explained to students is that Jesus did, in fact, die on the cross. If they have never been exposed to the common objections to the resurrection, some learners may feel as though an explanation of why we believe Jesus died is much ado about nothing. Simply expressing that Jesus' death is the first proposition of Paul's gospel presentation in 1 Corinthians 15 should suffice as a reason for the discussion. There are only three evidences to which students need to point in order to make a beginner appeal to the death of Christ. First, they should simply point out that the vast majority of scholars accept Jesus' death by Roman crucifixion. Quotes, like the ones mentioned earlier in the chapter can be provided to demonstrate the truth of this claim. Second, students can explain how absurd the idea is that a Roman soldier would ever be mistaken about the death of his subject. Third, learners can point out that there are at least four documents describing the death of Jesus in the Bible and three from outside of the Bible covered in this chapter. This is evidence even if unbelievers do not see it as good evidence. Any claim that Jesus did not die by crucifixion is based on speculation and not a shred of documentary evidence.

Conclusion

In this chapter we have considered the evidence that the crucifixion was fatal for Jesus. This means that the "F." in F.A.C.T.S. should be understandable for learners at this point. With the information provided herein, facilitators should be able to train a class of believers or seekers in the truth of "F." Furthermore, readers should now see that atheist scholars, like Gerd Ludemann and renowned Christian thinkers like N.T. Wright, find the idea that Jesus somehow survived or evaded the crucifixion to be completely indefensible. We have seen the reasons for this. Moreover, we have multiple independent attestation to the event in the gospels and writings of Paul. Jesus' wounds on the cross were FATAL. This means we are ready to move on and discuss the appearances.

Questions

1. Why does the "F." in C.O.R.E. F.A.C.T.S. stand for *Fatal*?
2. What is the swoon (apparent death) theory?
3. What do Roman soldiers have to do with this issue?
4. What historical evidence from the Bible do we have that Jesus died?
5. What historical evidence from outside of the Bible do we have that Jesus died?
6. What seems to be wrong with the claim that Christians are just biased?

CHAPTER VI

A

JESUS **APPEARED** TO OTHERS AFTER HIS DEATH

After that he appeared to more than five hundred brethren
at one time—1 Corinthians 15:6

Introduction

Though we have mounted up evidence for Jesus' death by Roman crucifixion, we would be mistaken to call him Lord if he remained in the tomb. However, that Jesus appeared to others after his death is greatly evidenced as well. In this chapter we will examine this evidence and consider what leaders in the relevant fields have to say about it. While the majority of scholars agree that followers and enemies of the faith believed that Jesus had APPEARED to them as the risen Lord, this is still one of the most controversial aspects of the investigation.

A strong case can be made for the resurrection from 1 Corinthians 15. As cited later in this chapter, skeptical scholars agree that a portion of this passage is valid material for making cases like this. After all, the letter itself has an unarguably early date and, most agree, was in fact written by Paul. In that letter Paul claims that Jesus died, was buried and later rose again. He explains,

> Moreover, brethren, I declare unto you the gospel which
> I preached unto you, which also ye have received, and
> wherein ye stand; By which also ye are saved, if ye keep in

memory what I preached unto you, unless ye have believed in vain. For I delivered unto you first of all that which I also received, how that Christ died for our sins according to the scriptures; And that he was buried, and that he rose again the third day according to the scriptures[43]

Apologists are justified in using the Bible itself to make this argument. I realize that it is circular reasoning to use some *thing* to prove that same *thing;* although in this case, testimony of Christ's resurrection is logically defensible. Moreover, 1 Corinthians 15:3-5b is accepted by even the liberal, barely-religious *Jesus Seminar* as authentic and true. This leads us to address one of the great criticisms of the resurrection case.

CORE MOMENT

Beginners don't really need to know about The Jesus Seminar. Just know that even those biblical scholars who are most skeptical of the bodily resurrection of Jesus still grant that certain biblical passages are historically reliable. The point is that if even enemies of Christianity admit that a verse is true, then there is really no reason to doubt it.

It is often argued that by the time Paul penned his letters, there had been sufficient years for the facts to get distorted and a simple story to become mythical. That is to say, at the time of the events surrounding Jesus' life, people knew that he did not really die and rise again, but over time the story grew more and more fantastic. The truth is that the Scripture that is agreed upon by even non-Christian scholars

---

[43] 1 Corinthians 15:1-4—I have quoted this from the KJV because its translation has been the one addressed by most biblical critics.

demonstrates that individuals were claiming the resurrection of Christ from the dead immediately after the events took place.

CORE MOMENT

What follows below is kind of technical, but don't worry. All we're doing is showing that the facts about the resurrection were believed by Christians from the very end of Jesus' earthly ministry. This is important because it means that the stories of the appearances didn't just spring up as fairy tales decades later.

It is agreed among most scholars that the statements about Christ's death, burial and resurrection as recorded in 1 Corinthians 15:3-5b are in the form of a creedal statement that was likely intended for use by the community of Christians.[44] Paul claims, in the third verse, that he received it from someone else, but he does not share who that was. However, the only possibility that we find in his writings is his visit to the church in Jerusalem described in Galatians 1:18. According to this passage, the meeting took place three years after his conversion on the road to Damascus. Since most scholars place Paul's conversion between one and three years after the events surrounding the crucifixion, this would date Paul's reception of the creed in 1 Corinthians 15 to just between four and six years after those events. Since it was already a creedal statement in use by the church at that point, it must have originated prior to Paul's reception of it. This means that we have solid evidence based on Scripture, that is permitted even by enemies of Christianity, that almost immediately after Christ left the earth people were claiming regularly that he had died, was buried and rose again. Thus, there is internal evidence in Scripture that makes

---

[44] See objection: "What if the resurrection is spiritual rather than physical?"

the idea that Christianity became more mythical as time went on, outlandish. Strikingly, this is not the only evidence on hand.

Paul claimed in the above passage that Jesus died, was buried and rose from the grave. Imagine that the same thing was claimed about the president. Most would think this was foolishness. But what if researchers were able to locate over five hundred people who all testified that he truly had? What if they all stood in a courtroom and gave the same report about the same event, though they were scattered all over the country and did not correspond? The argument would be difficult to refute. This is exactly what is represented in Paul's statements. He claimed,

> And that he was seen of Cephas, then of the twelve: After that, he was seen of above five hundred brethren at once; of whom the greater part remain unto this present, but some are fallen asleep. After that, he was seen of James; then of all the apostles. And last of all he was seen of me also, as of one born out of due time.[45]

Paul said that Jesus was seen after his resurrection alive and well. He wasn't seen by ten, fifty or one hundred. Jesus was seen in several different locations by over five hundred people who were all willing to testify to the event. Thus, Jesus died, and later appeared to others alive and well.

---

[45]   1 Corinthians 15:5-8

Objections

CORE MOMENT

These objections can get kind of technical. If you're a beginner, it might be a good idea to just focus on the actual evidence we've covered so far. You can always come back to these objections once you've grown in your understanding a little more. If you think you're ready then keep reading. Just don't get discouraged if it's tough at first.

What if Paul fabricated the appearances of Jesus?

Paul claimed in 1 Corinthians 15 that most of those who saw the risen Christ were still living at the time he wrote to the Corinthians. If Paul lied in a claim that was repeated world wide, mentioned specific names of people who saw the risen Lord, and that in one outstanding sociological event Christ revealed himself to five hundred people, shouldn't there be someone who refuted this? Indeed, wouldn't the Jewish leadership that was so opposed to Christianity find Israelites who would deny that a gathering of five hundred ever claimed to have seen such a thing? Wouldn't those whose names Paul mentioned speak out against him? Of the countless manuscripts that support Paul's claims, not one single trustworthy manuscript has ever been located anywhere in the world at any time stating that what Paul said was untrue.

Some might claim, "By the time Paul's letter to the Corinthians was circulated and reproduced those critics would be dead." Yet, this was a world in which verbal communication and written dialogue were paramount to a successful society. N.T. Wright demands, ". . . at a time when many regarded the spoken word as carrying more authority than the written, history as speaking-about-events-in-the-past is not to be sneezed at.'[46] The Hebrews are known for their verbal history. Even today, orthodox Jewish families pass on what they know of the past from one generation to the next with virtually no discrepancies. American men tell their kids they caught a catfish that weighed fifteen pounds and three weeks later it is reported that a catfish the size of a Volkswagen was pulled out of the lake. Hebrews are not like this. They are exact. Even if it could be said that the original critics were dead by the time Paul's letter had gained popularity, the offspring of those critics would have set the record straight. However, this is not likely. Most critics date 1 Corinthians as one of the earliest Pauline letters we have, probably written around 55 AD.

Lee Strobel, in his book, *The Case for Christ*,[47] explains that the testimony of this many witnesses would be an insurmountable case that the event was true. If each was given just fifteen minutes to give testimony and the court took no recess, it would take at least an entire week to hear each argument. Any jury would love to have that kind of assurance. This lends great weight to the case that the appearances were legitimate.

What if the disciples merely had visions, dreams or hallucinations of Jesus?

Because of the strong evidence for the death and later appearances of Jesus, some researchers have adopted the view that rather than actually encountering the real Jesus, early believers were experiencing some form of mental anomaly. The claim is that an admittedly highly unlikely and unusual event occurred in the New Testament at which multiple individuals experienced similar hallucinations, dreams or visions. This resulted in the mistaken belief on the part of first century

---

[46]   Wright, N.T., *The Resurrection of the Son of God*, (Minneapolis, MN: Fortress Press, 2003), 13.

[47]   Strobel, Lee, *The Case for Christ*, (Grand Rapids, MI: Zondervan, 1998), 237.

Christians that Jesus was indeed raised from the dead. This contention is manifested in a variety of forms. Either early Christians experienced individual hallucinations, group hallucinations or some sort of disorder based on their own grief.

Gerd Ludemann argues that the disciples, including the five hundred, experienced ecstatic mass hallucinations in which they were all convinced that they had seen Jesus alive because of religious expectation.[48] The problem with this hypothesis is that religious expectation would not result in a similar hallucination for the individuals of this specific crowd. The differences in their religious backgrounds, including differences from what Jesus taught, would have resulted in a wild variety of differing hallucinations. Moreover, any argument that a given event is merely a hallucination brought on by religious expectation is merely question begging unless the proponent can already demonstrate that the event was false by some other means.

In the cases of Paul, Peter and James, skeptics often argue that a mental phenomenon known as conversion disorder was at play. Conversion disorder is a problem experienced by individuals who have a serious and dramatic onslaught of emotional distress. If, to illustrate, Paul suddenly recognized the horror that he had been persecuting and killing individuals for practicing a strange offshoot of Judaism, he might experience blindness or paralysis (both of which are symptoms of conversion disorder).[49]

The problems with this hypothesis are apparent. First, even if one could explain the events of Paul's testimony by appealing to this strange and rare disorder, it would say nothing of the hundreds of others who claimed to have seen the raised Jesus. Second, when Paul describes his former life, we are painted a picture of a guiltless,

---

[48]   Ludemann, Gerd, *The Resurrection of Jesus,* (Amherst, NY: Prometheus, 2009), 106,107

[49]   Borowski, Maria, "Conversion Disorder," (http://www.med.nyu.edu/content?ChunkIID=96743) Internet. Accessed on 27 July, 2012.

cavalier crusader.[50] That Paul was grief-stricken is narrated nowhere in his writings prior to the events of his conversion itself. With respect to Peter and James, critics are relying on even less evidence. In brief, just because something could have been the case does not mean that it was the case, in fact. This argument is merely *ad hoc*.

CORE MOMENT

The idea that those who claimed to have seen Jesus risen from the dead were all experiencing a hallucination is based on zero evidence. This is an example of stretching as far as you can to avoid having to accept the truth.

What if the resurrection was spiritual rather than physical?

This objection requires some extended and intricate evaluation. The skeptical group of liberal scholarship known as The Jesus Seminar has argued in favor of this position regularly. The view of The Jesus Seminar regarding the resurrection of Jesus is primarily that if it occurred, it was metaphorical rather than physical in nature. That is to say that various scholars within the Seminar do not view the resurrection as having occurred in any sense, but no scholar seems to affirm that the resurrection was physical in nature. This becomes blatant when reading what Jesus Seminar founder, Robert Funk, claims about the body of Jesus, "His body may have been left to rot on the cross, to become carrion for dogs and crows. What we have come to call the resurrection (by a kind of theological short-hand) is nowhere narrated directly except in the highly imaginative account in the Gospel of Peter."[51] Clearly Funk denies a bodily resurrection, but what

---

[50] Acts 22:1-5

[51] Funk, Robert, *Honest to Jesus: Jesus for a New Millenium*, (San Francisco, CA: Harper, 1997), 219.

of his compatriots? Other figures among the most well known in the Seminar have made similar claims which narrow the scope of what the resurrection could have been. Marcus Borg,[52] John Dominic Crossan,[53] Gerd Ludemann[54] and Robert Price[55] all claim that when one observes the evidence regarding the historical Jesus, only naturalism appears on the surface. While many of them urge Christians that this does not rob the faith of the meaning of the resurrection, they do agree as a Seminar that it is not the bodily resurrection of orthodox Christianity. Undeniably this is a bold claim.

As they promote their view, The Jesus Seminar makes a case for the non-physicality of the resurrection by appealing to Scripture and historiographical precedence. Not only do the fellows envision a *prima facia* naturalistic Easter account, but they claim that Paul even understood the resurrected body of Jesus to be ethereal and spiritual rather than physical. In discussing Paul's words, Crossan and Borg write, "First he says there are many kinds of bodies (1 Cor. 15:38-41) Then, in a series of contrasts, he writes about the differences between physical bodies and resurrected bodies . . . The resurrected body, including the body of Jesus, is a spiritual body."[56]

Conversely, conservative evangelicals maintain the belief that the resurrection was indeed bodily in nature. Offering an apologetic in favor of the orthodox view, proponents of this position argue for the bodily resurrection of Jesus and the likewise future bodily resurrection of the saints by demonstrating that a proper hermeneutic and understanding of history leads one to the conclusion that the

---

52   Borg, Marcus; Crossan, John Dominic. *The First Paul*, (San Francisco, CA: HarperOne 1st edition, 2009), 151.

53   Ibid.

54   Ludemann, Gerd, *The Resurrection of Christ a Historical Inquiry*, (Amherst, NY: Prometheus, 2009), 189.

55   Price, Robert, T*he Incredible Shrinking Son of Man*, (Amherst, NY: Prometheus, 2003), 336.

56   Borg, Marcus; Crossan, John Dominic, *The First Paul*. (San Francisco, CA: HarperOne 1st edition, 2009), 151.

resurrection was physical. The specific arguments that bear this out will follow. Nevertheless, the manner in which apologists such as Gary Habermas present their defenses demonstrates that they are self-consciously aware of the assertions of The Jesus Seminar. That is to say, even when not debating with Jesus Seminar fellows, the arguments involve concessions made by the Seminar.

Habermas has become known for his minimal facts argument in favor of the resurrection of Jesus.[57] He crafts the argument in such a way that each fact is accepted by the majority of New Testament scholars including The Jesus Seminar. Most importantly, 1 Corinthians 15: 3b-5 is the launch pad from which Habermas begins and it is precisely the vital resurrection passage permitted by The Jesus Seminar as authentic in their book, "*The Five Gospels*." Therein the Seminar confesses, "The earliest version of the oral gospel preserved for us in written record is the 'gospel' Paul reports in 1 Cor 15:3-5."[58] With such an approach in mind, Christian apologists have recently sought to build a case for the bodily resurrection on the basis of only those passages granted by the Seminar, therefore, bypassing much of the debate. Moreover, conservative scholars maintain that viewing the resurrection as merely spiritual or metaphorical would not account for the change in and background of Jewish belief.

It should be said that there are those in the Seminar who would tread so far as to claim that Jesus may have never existed even as a mere human.[59] There are those in the conservative camp who claim that we can prove the bodily resurrection to almost a certainty. Norman Geisler claims, "Unlike most other religious worldviews, Christianity is built on historical events and can therefore be either proven or falsified by historical investigation. The problem for all

---

[57] Habermas, Gary & Licona, Michael, *The Case for the Resurrection of Jesus,* (Grand Rapids, MI:Kregel Press, 2004).

[58] Funk, Robert & The Jesus Seminar, *The Five Gospels*, (San Fransisco, CA: Polebridge Press, 1993), 24.

[59] Price, Robert. *The Incredible Shrinking Son of Man*, (Amherst, NY: Prometheus, 2003), 336.

the skeptics and critics is that all the evidence points toward the resurrection."[60] Yet, these are extremes indeed. They are mentioned because they place a magnifier on the matter. Nevertheless, it would be a mistake to conclude that these scholars are too accommodating. The disagreement is fierce. This may be in part because of their backgrounds.

One may wonder, "Why is there so much disagreement on issues as seemingly uncontroversial as how to do historical inquiry?" Taking a look at the guiding principles of The Jesus Seminar and those who oppose them may provide some light on their reasoning. In *The Five Gospels*, the Seminar provides some insight into the decision making process which they employed. A firestorm of controversy developed when these principles were originally published.

Regarding the very "first pillar of scholarly wisdom" set forth as a guiding principle in culling away material which does not reflect the true Jesus of history is to make a bifurcation between the Jesus of fact and the Jesus of faith. To articulate which items the Seminar recognizes as false it credits the idea of David Friedrich Strauss that one should disregard, ". . . the 'mythical' (defined by him as anything legendary or supernatural) . . ."[61] In this way the fellows hoped to successfully remove the fictitious ideas about Jesus that were incorporated into the gospels by later followers who, upon reflection, mythologized and romanticized the story. For a prime example of such embellishment, the group would direct readers to the obviously fabricated Jesus of the fourth gospel (The Gospel of John). Furthermore, the rejection of John constitutes their second pillar. It is their contention that John presents a thoroughly "spiritual" Jesus not found in the proper reading of the earlier synoptic gospels.[62] Little is given by way of a basis for the first pillar, save the implied validity of

---

60   Geisler, Norman; Turek, Frank, *I Don't Have Enough Faith to Be an Atheist*, (Wheaton, IL: Crossway Books, 2004), 374.

61   Funk, Robert & The Jesus Seminar, *The Five Gospels*, (San Fransisco, CA: Polebridge Press, 1993), 3.

62   Ibid.

Strauss' work for further reading, other than that it appears to be a bare assertion.

With respect to the second pillar, it is argued that the oral tradition will clearly be earlier and thus the Gospel of John normally dated, at the earliest, to the end of the first century would not have been directly based upon them. Moreover, the second pillar seems to be somewhat established on the basis of the first in that it contains a thoroughly "spiritual" Jesus. Conservative scholars wasted no time in responding to this, and still continue to articulate what they see as glaring difficulties with these first two pillars.

Responding to the first pillar, William Lane Craig demands, "Now this presupposition constitutes an absolute watershed for the study of the gospels. If you presuppose naturalism, then things like the incarnation, the Virgin Birth, Jesus' miracles, and his resurrection go out the window before you even sit down at the table to look at the evidence . . . In other words, skepticism about the gospels is not based on history, but on the presupposition of naturalism."[63] Gary Habermas echoes this concern and points out the ramifications that this has for the resurrection. Besides the obvious result that the resurrection couldn't have been a physical reanimation of the corpse of Jesus, The Jesus Seminar does not affirm any material from the resurrection narratives.[64] It would seem that the opponents of The Jesus Seminar would recognize this as a major bias in their project.

Eminent New Testament scholar, N.T. Wright, who has repeatedly responded to the Seminar (specifically Crossan) explains how he views this bias affecting their work on the Gospel of John, "But here we see quite sharply, what we shall observe in more detail presently: the Seminar's method has not been to examine each saying all by itself and decide about it, but to start with a fairly clear picture of Jesus

---

[63] Craig, William Lane, *Rediscovering the Historical Jesus: The Presuppositions and Pressumptions of The Jesus Seminar,* (*Faith and Mission,* 15 1998), 3-15.

[64] Habermas, Gary, *The Historical Jesus,* (Joplin, MO: College Press, 1996), 123.

and early Christianity, and simply run through the material imposing this picture on the texts."[65] According to Wright, the approach would have otherwise resembled a case by case examination of the words of Jesus rather than a wholesale rejection of what seems to conflict with a naturalistic understanding. Nevertheless, this discussion may beg the question, "Do these comments betray some unfounded presuppositions on the part of the conservative apologists?"

The Jesus Seminar makes no official defense of their claims that the "Jesus of faith" (the supernatural Jesus) should be rejected. However, they do claim, in stating their seventh pillar, that the burden of proof is now firmly on the part of those who posit such a Jesus. In this scientific age, the believer in the miraculous must demonstrate that the miraculous exists, or at the very least existed with respect to Jesus. Perhaps it is the case that the presupposition of naturalism on the part of The Jesus Seminar is no worse a sin than the apparent presupposition of the miraculous on the part of conservative scholars.

In response to this, Michael Licona demands that whether or not the historian (because he is not doing theology) is allowed to come to a theological conclusion, he must be allowed to consider the possibility of the miraculous if it is the most plausible explanation available. If it is the case that a divine miracle has occurred then excluding it as an option *a priori* negates the possibility of a successful account of the actual historical events. He claims, "If the resurrection of Jesus was an event that occurred, in history, those who refuse the historian the right to investigate it or who *a priori* exclude miracles as a possible answer could actually be placing themselves in a position where they cannot appraise history accurately."[66] This seems to be the position taken by conservatives in a general sense. Moreover, such scholars, whether the burden of proof is theirs or not, do attempt to respond to the challenges

---

[65]   Wright, N.T., *Authenticating the Activities of Jesus*, ed. Bruce Chilton and Craig A. Evans. (Boston, MA: Brill Press, 2002), 83-120.

[66]   Licona, Mike, *The Resurrection of Jesus: A New Historiographical Approach,* (Downers Grove, IL: Intervarsity Press, 2010), 198.

faced by them using biblical and historiographical argumentation, the former of which will be discussed below. However, the biases which may exist are clear.

On the one hand, The Jesus Seminar admittedly begins with an assertion which is, if not exactly, very similar to naturalism. This drives their operations to an end which is not unsurprising. Is it circular reasoning to begin in such a way and then conclude that nothing supernatural is true of the Jesus of orthodox Christianity? For Licona, Craig, and Habermas it certainly seems to be. Moreover, this philosophy seems to have a trickle-down effect on other guiding principles. As Habermas has stated, the discussion of John's Gospel is compromised from the outset because of this. Rather than a case by case approach to the sayings of Jesus, the bias against the supernatural has removed the very possibility that the author of John would receive a fair hearing. Conversely, these same apologists must face the taxing challenge of demonstrating that their belief in the miraculous is not a similar, albeit, antithetical bias.

The biblical data accepted as early authentic Christian material by both sides seems to be a reasonable measuring stick for determining whether the resurrection was a supernatural physiological raising of the dead or a mere meaningful metaphor. This places highly limiting parameters on the discussion since The Jesus Seminar has eliminated almost all resurrection material from the canon. Still, this limitation may serve as an asset for expediting the discussion. Thus, attention may now be paid to the teaching of the remaining resurrection account validated as an early oral creed of the Christian church.

As already stated above, the Seminar could not deny that the statements of 1 Corinthians 15:3-5b represent an early creedal statement which dates back to only a short time (certainly less than five years) after the Easter events. This is undisputed. The only remaining question is, "what did early believers mean by this?" Fellows of the Seminar have been quite outspoken on this issue.

Seminar fellow, Marcus Borg, provides four reasons why he believes that the resurrection mentioned in this passage is simply a metaphor. Namely, Paul makes no mention of the empty tomb, the verb translated "appeared" is often used in the New Testament in conjunction with visions, and Paul later claims that the resurrection body will be to regular bodies as plants are to the seeds from which they grow. He then concludes his discussion of the passage with a claim about verse fourteen. He asserts, "Verse 14 is often cited by our fundamentalist brothers and sisters in support of the absolute centrality of a physical resurrection . . . but the verse is found in a chapter that strongly suggests that the resurrection body is not a physical body."[67] These are serious challenges.

In evaluating these four contentions, the first point would turn out to be irrelevant if it is the case that the resurrection was bodily. That is to say, if he was dead, buried and then physically seen by others, then it goes without saying that there was an empty tomb. N.T. Wright makes the point, "The fact that the empty tomb itself, so prominent in the gospel accounts, does not appear to be specifically mentioned in this passage is not significant; the mention here of 'buried then raised' no more needs to be amplified in that way than one would need to amplify 'I walked down the street' with the qualification, 'on my feet.'"[68] Point number two is irrelevant in that one cannot import the way other New Testament authors used a word and assume that Paul meant it in the same way. His third claim seems to be a straw-man argument in that orthodox Christianity does not claim that the body of Jesus is exactly the same as it was prior to death. If nothing else, Jesus' resurrection body is immortal. Lastly, Borg's comment on verse fourteen relies on the truth of his first point which he is attempting to demonstrate, in part by the fourth point itself, rendering the argument circular. With

---

67 Borg, Marcus; Wright, N.T. *The Meaning of Jesus.* HarperCollins, (San Francisco, CA: Harper Collins, 2007), 132,133.
68 Wright, N.T., *The Resurrection of the Son of God*, (Minneapolis, MN: Fortress Press, 2003), 321.

respect to this debate, it would seem that the liberal scholar's argument will not stand. Yet, Borg is not the only critic of the orthodox position.

In making a case that the author of Mark fabricated the discovery of the empty tomb by a group of Jesus' women followers, John Dominic Crossan cites the creedal statement recorded by Paul as evidence that the empty tomb was not initially taught.[69] As already demonstrated by Wright, this speaks not to the emptiness of the tomb. Yet, it is noteworthy that Crossan seems to hold that by the supposed manufacturing of the story of the women by the author of Mark, the actuality of the empty tomb is rendered less probable. First, this is based upon the claim of the Jesus Seminar that the resurrection narratives are not reliable, which is likewise based upon the *ad hoc* assertion that such narratives be removed because they imply the miraculous. Secondly, there is enough internal evidence in the creedal statement to demonstrate that it was referring to a physical resurrection, according to Kirk MacGregor.

MacGregor finds the teaching of 1 Corinthians 15:3-5 to teach bodily, physical resurrection for at least one glaring reason. He claims that the Greek verb translated "raised" denotes this. He says, "Quite significantly, the verb εγείρω (lexical form of έγήγερται) means 'to cause to stand up from a lying or reclining position with the implication of some degree of previous incapacity.'"[70] He further argues that if the physical body of Jesus was raised and then the creed immediately refers to the appearances with no intermediate qualifier, one can only surmise that what was raised (the physical body of Jesus) was what was seen. On the basis of 1 Corinthians 15:3-5, therefore, it is difficult to accept anything but a bodily resurrected Jesus.

The Jesus Seminar has allowed for very little resurrection data from Christian Scripture. Yet, with what it has granted, conservative scholars

---

[69]   Crossan, John Dominic, *The Birth of Christianity*, (San Francisco, CA: HarperOne 1st ed., 1999), 551.

[70]   MacGregor, Kirk R. *1 Corinthians 15:3b-6a,7 and the bodily resurrection of Jesus*, (Journal of the evangelical theological society, 49 no 2 Je 2006), 230,231.

have convincingly developed a case for the resurrection based on proper biblical interpretation. Thus, from the biblical data one would be justified in accepting the position of these conservative evangelicals. It appears that according to the Bible, as approved by The Jesus Seminar, the earliest Christians held to a bodily resurrection. This means that the appearances must be understood as physical appearances.

CORE MOMENT

Give your brain a rest. Beginners don't need to know all the ins and outs of what was just explained. I only included it because the bodily resurrection is so central to evangelical Christian belief.

Transitioning the Presentation for the Layman

The "A." in "F.A.C.T.S. represents the "appearances" of Jesus to onlookers. Facilitators can explain to students that most scholars admit that hundreds of individuals truly believed that Jesus had appeared to them alive. This will be backed up by further evidence when facilitators explain "C.," but the issue which needs to be driven home is that Jesus' death and then subsequent appearing to others alive is powerful evidence in favor of the resurrection hypothesis. As supplementary evidence, facilitators could reference the rapid expansion of the early church. Unlike the many false cults of the day, Christianity would not be stomped out despite consecutive persecutions.

Conclusion

The "A." in C.O.R.E. F.A.C.T.S. is one of the most vital aspects of the case. In this chapter we have covered the subject of the appearances of Jesus specifically as they are recorded by Paul in 1 Corinthians 15. Major objections were discussed in a fair amount of detail. Because of the seriousness of the bodily nature of the resurrection for Christian doctrine, I spent a considerable amount of time explaining why readers should draw the conclusion that the resurrection of Jesus was a physical one. This point can be easily learned by students for evangelistic purposes and should always be included in an apologetic case for the resurrection. On the basis of this evidence, we may rightly assert that Jesus *Appeared* bodily after his death.

Questions

1. Why does the "A." in C.O.R.E. F.A.C.T.S. stand for *Appeared*?
2. In what biblical passage does Paul argue for the truth of the resurrection?
3. Give at least one good reason a proper interpretation indicates a bodily resurrection.
4. How do secular scholars explain the appearances of Jesus?
5. How can the case for the appearances be summarized?
6. Why are the appearances of Jesus so significant for the case for the resurrection?

CHAPTER VII

C

THE DISCIPLES WERE **COMMITTED** TO THE POINT OF DEATH

And on that day a great persecution began against the church in Jerusalem, and they were all scattered throughout the regions.—Acts 8:1

Introduction

Now that we have established that Jesus' wounds on the cross were fatal, and that individuals were claiming that he appeared to them bodily after his death, it is time to consider even further evidence that these claims are true by examining the commitment level of those who made them. Though this chapter amounts to only one of several necessary steps in demonstrating the truth of the resurrection, it refers to the evidence that may be the most powerful of all.

The Evidence

Perhaps the strongest data for the validity of the resurrection is the truth that men will not die for a lie. Church tradition holds that each of the apostles died a martyr's death for preaching the resurrection of Christ with the exception of John, who was boiled in oil and then banished to Patmos. Modern investigators, however, cannot demonstrate with absolute certainty if, or how, all of the disciples were martyred, but we can say with absolute assurance that they were *willing* to die. The only group who would have benefited from hiding the body of Jesus would have been the apostles. The Jewish leaders and the Romans both wanted an end to the chaos surrounding the life and death of Jesus of Nazareth. So the question remains, "Why would these men all die for something they knew to be untrue?" Men will live for a lie, but they will not die for one under any circumstances. Remember, these disciples were all from different walks of life and it is prohibitively unlikely that they were all brainwashed. Even if they were lunatics, the fact remains that they would have seen the dead body of their former leader. Gary Habermas explains,

> Remember that their continual willingness to suffer and even die for those beliefs indicates that they sincerely regarded their beliefs as being true . . . People may die for what they believe is true, but it is not reasonable to think that an entire group of men would be willing to suffer horribly and die for something they all knew was false.[71]

Likewise, J.P. Moreland explains,

> The disciples had nothing to gain by lying and starting a new religion. They faced hardship, ridicule, hostility, and martyr's deaths. In light of this, they could never have sustained such unwavering motivation if they knew what they were preaching was a lie. The disciples were not fools and Paul was a cool-headed intellectual of the first rank. There would have been several opportunities over three to four decades of ministry to reconsider and renounce a lie.[72]

---

[71]   Habermas, Gary & Licona, Michael, *The Case for the Resurrection of Jesus*, (Grand Rapids, MI: Kregel Press, 2004), 200.

[72]   Moreland, J.P., *Scaling the Secular City*, (Grand Rapids, MI: Baker Books, 1987), 171,172.

Produce one man in history who has ever died for something he knew to be untrue for no recognizable reason and you will have an argument. Some would site the suicide bombers of extremist Muslim terrorists, but extremist Muslims truly believe in what they are dying for. The difference is that they are not eyewitnesses who know for sure whether their religion is true or false. Others might site lunatics like Jim Jones, but these cultic leaders were insane. If the resurrection did not really happen the apostles would have *known* that they were dying for a lie, and men just do not do that.

Objection

CORE MOMENT

These objections can get kind of technical. If you're a beginner, it might be a good idea to just focus on the actual evidence we've covered so far. You can always come back to these objections once you've grown in your understanding a little more. If you think you're ready then keep reading. Just don't get discouraged if it's tough at first.

How do we know that early Christians died for their beliefs?

This contention is an attempt to undercut the claim that the disciples (or early Christians) were committed even to the point of death. However, this is a misunderstanding of the claim. Though a historian would be hard-pressed to deny that they were martyred for what they believed, the case that we make for "C." hinges on the truth that these believers were *willing* to die for their belief. This may seem like a subtle difference, but we are able to conclude that members of the church were willing to die for what they believed. In chapter five, I cited Cornelius Tacitus' assertion that Nero blamed the Christians for the burning of Rome. This alone demonstrates their persecution. Moreover, these persecutions are so well documented in[73] and outside[74] of the Bible that the burden of proof would be on a skeptic to show that they did not occur.

Transitioning the Presentation for the Layman

"C." is for "commitment" because of the strong commitment level of early believers. They were willing to die for their beliefs in the resurrection. When explaining this to students I often choose one of them as an example. I ask,

> What if we all wanted to make up a religion here tonight? We might claim that Mr. Pollard was shot by an intruder and lay dead for thirty minutes before resurrecting. Let's imagine that the bullet hole closed before our very eyes. After the news found out about it we might all be asked to appear on a national morning news program. Now the religion which has come to be called "Pollardianism" is born. The story might catch on and some of us would begin to write books on the subject. Those of us sitting here tonight could soon become wealthy and famous. Now imagine a man catching you in a dark alley, placing a gun to your head and demanding that you admit the truth or else you will be killed. I think we would quickly abandon our Pollardian beliefs.

This is true because men will live for a lie as long as it might mean money, sex or power. When such attractive benefits begin to evaporate

---

[73] Acts 7:59,60, Acts 8:1-4, Acts 12:1,2,

[74] Josephus, Flavius, *The Antiquities of the Jews*, (Book XX Chapter Nine., Eusebius, *Historia Ecclesiastica*).

and are replaced by the prospect of death, people find it difficult to maintain their deceit.

Some further explanation will almost certainly be necessary. In a post-911 world, the question of Muslim extremists, so willing to give up their lives for Islam springs immediately to the minds of listeners. However, the differences outlined earlier in this chapter should be easy enough for facilitators to express.

Conclusion

In this short chapter it has been shown that the disciples of Jesus, including many members of the early church, were willing to suffer horribly because of their belief in the truth of the resurrection. Their willingness to suffer even extended to the point of death. Men may live for a lie, but they will not die for one. This can be easily expressed to learners by comparison. Thus, the *Commitment* level of the followers of Jesus counts as powerful evidence for the truth of the resurrection.

Questions

1. Why does the "C." in C.O.R.E. F.A.C.T.S. stand for *Committed*?
2. Explain the statement, "Men will live for a lie, but they will not die for one."
3. Why is the commitment level of the early church different from modern Muslim faith?
4. What is wrong with the claim that the disciples were just brainwashed?
5. Explain the analogy of "Pallardianism."
6. How can one summarize the case that the disciples were so *Committed*?

CHAPTER VIII

THE **TESTIMONY** OF MAN IS THAT JESUS WAS RAISED

He is not here, but he has risen. Remember how he spoke to you while he was still in Galilee—Luke 24:6

Introduction

At this point we are prepared to consider the testimony of mankind regarding the resurrection of Jesus. Doing so will demonstrate the centrality of the Christian faith for the flow of human history. First, we will consider the mark that Jesus has left on planet earth. This data must be accepted whether one recognizes Jesus as Lord or not. Involved in this will be an analysis of how the citizens of the modern western world seem to react to the character of Jesus. Second, we will consider the testimony of the gospels themselves. Are they truly reliable? If so, it must be determined whether their testimony is consistent with what the early church was proclaiming in its earliest days. Third, we will consider whether the views of today's skeptical scholars confirm the points we have been addressing throughout the last three chapters, and finally we will consider objections to the case.

CORE FACTS

Don't get distracted! We'll look at a lot of interesting material in this chapter but the most important emphasis is that the believer should be prepared to share his own testimony of his relationship with Jesus. If you're a skeptic, this is a great chance to consider the testimony of the world about Jesus.

The Testimony of World History

Having never traveled far from his birthplace, written a single document, run for political office, taken a wife, fathered any heirs or even spoken up for himself in the face of injustice, Jesus of Nazareth is the most influential human being who has ever been born. This alone should be enough to leave observers inquiring as to what the life and teaching of the historical Jesus actually were. Whether Christian, Muslim, Jewish, Hindu, atheist or agnostic, men of every persuasion and cultural origin have attempted to fully explore the story of the man and determine why his influence was so far spread. Why have thinkers throughout history taken the story of Christ so seriously?

Even the most venomous and hate-filled opponents of Christ's church find it difficult to speak ill of the man himself. Even though he warned the world of the reality of hell,[75] introduced a view of morality in which even the thoughts of man can be evil and preached that he alone was the way to obtain everlasting life,[76] people who live contrary to his teachings are wary of doing any violence to his name. Naturally, sinners throughout history, in an attempt to accommodate their own shortcomings, have twisted the words of Jesus to sound as though he was more permissive of unrighteousness than he was, but they still

---

[75]   Luke 12
[76]   John 14

find it offensive to disregard him outright. What was so amazing about this Christ that we find in him a nature that is absolutely unobjectionable?

Having spoken in churches around the world, I have often delivered less offensive messages than Jesus and yet been labeled a hell-fire-and-brimstone preacher by individuals who seem entirely ignorant of his difficult teachings on this matter. On occasion, I have been told, "Jesus just wouldn't have talked about hell," or "Jesus wouldn't have said he was the only way to heaven." Such statements not only demonstrate a lack of biblical knowledge, but they also show that many hearers are fully prepared to shoot the messenger while defending its sender. Would it not be easier to simply abandon the teachings of Christ? Indeed many have, but others find it impossible to treat him in any other way than kingly. Again, we find ourselves asking, "What is still so impressive about this man that we cannot deny him?"

His teachings have been dissected by scholars throughout Christian history. What might cause educated men to take his message so seriously that religious and national divisions have resulted from varying interpretations? Even during the third, fourth and fifth centuries there were already major churches in Jerusalem, Alexandria, Rome, Constantinople, Antioch and elsewhere, with each community slightly differing on points of theological significance. This had obvious political ramifications making Christianity not merely a matter important to faith but to the governance of mankind as well. Rounding out the relevance of Jesus' message to the whole of human experience, faithful believers who credited Christ with their work made scientific discoveries, began scientific institutions, and established hospitals as a result. Clearly the message of Christ has had a dramatic impact on every aspect of the human life. I believe this is because he is, in fact, the Lord of all creation.

Could it be that the message of Jesus is of such great importance because the events surrounding his death demonstrate that he was speaking the words of the divine? That is to say, could it be that Jesus' message retains its power for us because he is the one person in the history of humanity to have passed through the doorway of death, allowed it to shut firmly behind him and three days later walked back through it to explain everything to hundreds of onlookers?

Such an idea is often dismissed by skeptics outright. Hard pressed are we to find many people of sound mind today who claim to have ever encountered someone who has returned from death. Where such a person is found, we find ourselves hopelessly doubtful of their claims. I have often asked congregants of local churches whether they believed that Jesus had risen from the dead. Without question almost every hand will rise, but when I follow by asking, "Has anyone ever witnessed such a resurrection?" I never render from the audience an affirmation.

Rejoicing is in order for the faith of the believer; still this demonstrates two things. First, it shows that very intelligent people in the Christian faith believe something that seems extremely unlikely. There must be some good reason for their acceptance of these teachings. This is not, in itself, an argument that Jesus rose from the dead. Rather, it is yet another of the examples we have been considering of how this simple carpenter has impacted learned and unlearned people since the time of his preaching. Since the enlightenment emphasis on rationality in epistemology, it is unlikely that all of these believers would take such a divine claim seriously unless they had some reason for doing so. Second, the fact demonstrates that unbelievers have a good reason to ask questions. Even if Jesus truly died and rose again, and those who were his contemporaries were witnesses of it, we are still left wondering what valid reason we have in the 21st century for buying into his claims. After all, we stand two thousand years after the time of the supposed Messiah and surely there cannot be much left to convince us.

If Jesus has returned from the grave, any good reason to believe this is not only disintegrated beneath the dirt of the ancient world, but contrary to our present experience. Why then should we accept this claim as anything more than what we hear from opposing ancient religions? It seems that the only way to make sense of what modern believers think about Christ is to assume that they take it all on blind faith. Nevertheless, what if this is not so?

What if it truly is the case that there is good reason to believe that Jesus lives today? Wouldn't this be utterly life changing for anyone who recognized such a truth? Obviously, believers take the claims of Christ so seriously that they do more than simply mentally agree with him. They tend to change their lives. This is not to say that they are somehow perfect people, but believers throughout history begin to attempt the modification of the way they treat themselves and others. Furthermore, they change the way they view the person of Christ. No longer is he some ancient rabbi of minimal consequence, but he is alive. Springing forth from this belief of his present existence, Christians recognize a need to pray to him, thank him for his sacrifice for their sins, and live lives of gratitude. What is more, if his resurrection is evidence that he is the God of Scripture, then believers see him as the object of worship.

This is exactly what we see when we look at the position of the church. Atheists often point out the differences between Christian communities, but they fail to recognize that almost all mainstream groups do share certain issues that are of fundamental importance. Since its inception, the true church has recognized Jesus as being the way of salvation and the only hope for reaching the Father.

Let's consider what we have before us so far. In Jesus we find a man, the likes of which would commonly not have been influential, but who has influenced the world for two thousand years to the extent that his followers have shaped it in amazing ways. They have changed the courses of nations, inspired major technological advances, devoted their lives to his service, worshipped him as God, combed through his teachings as though they were the words of God and demonstrated that they were willing to die to defend the truth of his message. Ultimately, the community of faith has done this because of the central claim of the Christian faith; namely, that Jesus was raised by the Father from the dead.

Yet, as we have said, the hope of the believer is misplaced unless Jesus really has done what Christians claim that he has. If he merely died and remained dead, then there is no hope. If Jesus' resurrection did not take place, then his life came to an end as any other man. The ramifications of this are abundant, for not only would this mean that he died, but Augustine's *City of God* would become like any other kingdom in history. Ultimately, it would fall to the foreign invaders of some other faith, and indeed if it is built on a lie then it should.

Maybe Jesus was out of his mind. Certainly we are not at a loss of lunatics throughout history who have functioned as radical and insane leaders, but good psychology doesn't show this. Jesus displayed no signs of insanity. Even at the turning of tables, there seems to have been a time of consideration and planning before he proceeded. He had no desire for great power. Surely he wanted people to follow him, but even his disciples were disillusioned that he did not come to establish an earthly kingdom. Besides, many times he finished his miracles by telling people to remain quiet about what they had seen. Finally, his message was one of peace. He did not encourage mass suicide, sexual orgies, holy homicide or hatred of any person. Psychologists today should conclude that Jesus was a sane man. Imagine what it would mean if this were untrue.

Jesus made such a mark on planet earth that belief in him is still changing people for the better as no drug, counselor or psychological therapy is able to do. No reference for this is needed. Almost everyone knows someone who has altered their way of living because they have converted to a Christian lifestyle.

What we have been arguing here is basically that not only was Jesus a man of incredible influence but also a man to whom the charge of insanity or dishonesty will not stick. C.S. Lewis believed that this was great evidence for the divine nature of Jesus. His argument is referred to as the "trilemma." Lewis explains it thusly,

I am trying here to prevent anyone saying the really foolish thing that people often say about Him: 'I'm ready to accept Jesus as a great moral teacher, but I don't accept His claim to be God.' That is one thing we must not say. A man who was merely a man and said the sort of thing Jesus said would not be a great moral teacher. He would either be a lunatic—on a level with the man who says he is a poached egg—or else he would be the Devil of Hell. You must make your choice. Either this man was, and is, the Son of God: or else a madman or something worse. You can shut Him up for a fool, you can spit at Him and kill him as a demon or you can fall at his feet and call Him Lord and God. But let us not come with any patronizing nonsense about His being a great human teacher. He has not left that open to us. He did not intend to.[77]

What Lewis was trying to convey was the fact of Jesus' Lordship by process of elimination.

Often in today's culture we hear individuals referring to Jesus as a good moral teacher. By this they mean to stay faithful to the idea that he was a good man but not the God-man. This becomes problematic for Lewis in that it does not seem that one can logically say that Jesus was a good man and nothing more. As the above quote indicates, Jesus is either a lunatic if he really thought he was God, a liar if he was trying to deceive men about this, or he was Lord if it was true. If he was not a lunatic, then he must have either been a liar or the Lord. If he was not a liar, then he must have been a lunatic or Lord, and if he was not Lord, then he must have been a lunatic or a liar. Yet, none of these possibilities leave the idea of Jesus as simply a good man open to us as a live option.

---

[77] Lewis, C.S., *The Complete C.S. Lewis Signature Classics*, (San Francisco, CA: Harper Collins, 2002), 36.

Where this gets even more interesting is when one considers which of these three titles seems most attributable to him. Based on the evidence above, it does not seem rational to picture him as a lunatic. Moreover, he could not have been a liar and yet retained the good moral character that even unbelievers wish to ascribe to him. His identity is then left as nothing less than the Lord of all creation. Perhaps you can see the attraction of the trilemma. Most people are not prepared to condemn Jesus as a lunatic or a liar. However, if they are to deny the Lordship of Christ, then they must relegate him to one of these categories.

It should be noted that the trilemma argument is usually only persuasive if one of two things is true. If an individual is not willing to grant that the gospel record is trustworthy, then they will likely not be persuaded by this sort of presentation. Only an individual who already grants this will find value in the argument. Second, the argument might be helpful after evidence for the validity of Scripture has been established. If an apologist presents good evidence for the trustworthiness of the gospels, it is reasonable that he might move forward and advance Lewis' case. The only point *I* am putting forth *here* is that on the basis of what we do have, Jesus appears to be an honest and well-balanced individual. This claim is based on *some* evidence, even if critics do not trust the biblical record. Any claim that he was mentally imbalanced would be based on *zero* evidence.

The Testimonies of the Gospels

One of the tools for determining history properly is called multiple attestation. For obvious reasons, the more witnesses one is able to collect data from, the stronger a case can be made that a given event actually occurred. Critics of the Christian message recognize and advocate the use of this principle. Noted agnostic scholar, Bart Ehrman writes,

> I have repeatedly stressed that a tradition appearing in
> multiple, independent sources has a greater likelihood of
> being historically reliable than a tradition that appears in
> only one . . . If it is found independently in a number of
> sources, the probability of its being reliable is increased,
> assuming, of course, that it is contextually credible.[78]

Despite the fact that a strong case can be made in favor of the resurrection merely from 1 Corinthians 15, historians find multiple attestation in the gospels. Since these documents can be reasonably believed to have been written within the first century, they are strong sources for our consideration.

Many critics discount the gospels for varying reasons. One common complaint is that the gospels should not count as evidence in favor of the resurrection because they represent individuals who clearly had a bias in favor of Christianity. Nevertheless, there are at least two reasons why this charge will not stick. First, proponents of such an idea fail to recognize the value of seeking out primary source material. The gospels are among the primary sources on the life and teachings of Jesus. Historians pursuing terminal degrees would never graduate if they refused to consider the earliest sources available with respect to a particular historical matter. Why should the rules change when it comes to historical documents related to the life of Jesus? After all, the fact that they are the primary sources is why they were included in the canon of Scripture. F.F. Bruce explains,

> One thing must be emphatically stated. The New Testament
> books did not become authoritative for the Church because
> they were formally included in a canonical list; on the
> contrary, the Church included them in her canon because
> she already regarded them as divinely inspired, recognizing

---

[78] Ehrman, Bart, *Did Jesus Exist: The Historical Argument for Jesus of Nazareth*, (New York, NY: HarperCollins, 2012), 290.

their innate worth and generally apostolic authority, direct or indirect.[79]

Second, the implication is that the only sources that should be considered are those written by disinterested third parties. However, looking for a non-Christian source which contains an eyewitness account of the resurrection would be a fruitless search. It would be like looking for eyewitness testimony regarding a traffic accident from someone who witnessed the accident but does not believe it actually happened. For these reasons, it is fair to include the gospels in the discussion. John Warwick Montgomery demands, "To be skeptical of the resultant text of the New Testament books is to allow all of classical antiquity to slip into obscurity, for no documents of the ancient period are as well attested bibliographically as the New Testament."[80]

The principle of embarrassment

> **CORE MOMENT**
>
> I know this sounds like some complicated tool of scholarship but don't worry. The principle of embarrassment helps historians determine if something in a document is true. If someone who was claiming to be writing history records information that would be embarrassing, then he's probably telling the truth.

The veracity of the gospels is equally debated. How do historians in the 21st century judge such a document? The honesty of the authors

---

[79] Bruce, F.F., *The New Testament Documents*, (Charleston, SC: CreateSpace, 5th ed., 2011), 20.

[80] Montgomery, John Warwick, *History and Christianity*, (Minneapolis, MN: Bethany House, 1986), 29.

is of the utmost interest. One important tool historians use is known as the principle of embarrassment. If an author includes something that is personally embarrassing, then this counts in favor of the event as having actually happened and the author as retelling it honestly. We find this throughout the gospels. Women, for example, are the discoverers of the empty tomb. This was a patriarchal culture in which the testimony of a woman was considered to be greatly inferior to that of a man. If the authors were fabricating or embellishing the story, it is highly unlikely that they would have imagined the women followers of Jesus as the discoverers of the empty tomb.[81]

Moreover, Jesus is recorded as saying that he is unaware of the day or hour of his return. Habermas points out,

> It is unlikely that an author would invent an account so as to include the details that are embarrassing and potentially discrediting. In Mark 13:32, the gospel writer states that there is something Jesus does not know, the time of his coming. One would think that in an evolving theology where Jesus was assigned a divine status, even of being God himself, a statement emphasizing his limitations of knowledge would not be included. This is why most scholars agree that this verse is an actual statement of Jesus.[82]

Believers are able to explain why this is the case without difficulty, but if the story were deceptively constructed it would not have included this seemingly embarrassing fact about its protagonist. Finally, the disciples are found regularly confused by Jesus' teachings[83] and

---

[81] Licona, Mike, *The Resurrection of Jesus: A New Historiographical Approach,* (Downers Grove, IL: Intervarsity Press, 2010), 350.

[82] Habermas, Gary & Licona, Michael, *The Case for the Resurrection of Jesus,* (Grand Rapids, MI: Kregel Press, 2004), 169.

[83] Luke 24:25-27, 44-45; John 13:21-29.

hopelessly at a loss following his death.[84] None of these are the sorts of details one would expect to find in a fabricated story.

Multiple attestation

CORE MOMENT

The more sources that confirm the same event, the greater the likelihood that the event is true. If someone tells you that the Queen of England has been assassinated you might believe them. If 10 people tell you that the Queen has been assassinated, you are more likely to believe them.

Some point out that there appear to be contradictions between the gospel accounts. Bart Ehrman demands, "The Bible is filled with discrepancies, many of them irreconcilable contradictions."[85] Nevertheless, one must understand that the way modern thinkers report history is strikingly different from the way it was recorded in the first century. If the gospels are in the form of Greco-Roman biography, as they appear to be,[86] it was quite common to rearrange the chronology of events and explain how certain things happened in varying ways. Thus, what we might refer to as problems, bad form or contradictions amount to 21st century historians forcing their views of historiography onto a first century paradigm. These were not problems for historians working in the ancient world. Besides, many of the alleged contradictions reveal themselves to be nothing of the kind even by modern standards. One author reports that there is "an angel" at the tomb of Jesus, whereas another author reports more than one angel

---

84   John 20:19; John 18:13-27; John 20:24-29

85   Ehrman, Bart, *Jesus Interrupted: Revealing the Hidden Contradictions in the Bible*, (New York, NY: HarperCollins, 2009), 5.

86   Licona, Mike, *The Resurrection of Jesus: A New Historiographical Approach*, (Downers Grove, IL: Intervarsity Press, 2010), 34.

at the tomb of Jesus. It does not take much thought to work out that when you find more than one angel, it is true to say that there was "an angel" present. Lastly, though I would never concede that there are contradictions in Scripture, even if there were, it would not mean that the historical document in question was not trustworthy.

Differences between the documents may even increase the trustworthiness of those documents. If, for instance, four alleged conspiring thieves were asked to recount the events of the night of the theft, a word for word identical testimony would be damning. This would be evidence that they had agreed on a party-line. If our suspects were innocent, investigators would hear slightly differing details, while the major facts would be the same. Thus, any way a critic spins the story, the gospels count as valid source material for doing work on history. If these texts represent trustworthy authorship, then historians can consider the resurrection of Jesus to include multiple attestation.

Enemy attestation

CORE MOMENT

If the opponents of a given position affirm a fact that supports that position, then it is more likely to be true.

Another mark in favor of events having happened is known as enemy attestation. Habermas illustrates this principle thusly:

> If your mother says you are an honest person, we may have
> reason to believe her, yet with reservation, since she loves
> you and is somewhat biased. However, if someone who
> hates you admits that you are an honest person, we have

a stronger reason to believe what is being asserted since potential bias does not exist.[87]

If a document authored by someone who is, or was, hostile to the cause of another historical figure concedes the truth of his enemy's claims, then the probability that the events in question are true is raised. This is found in the testimony of Paul who had previously persecuted the church and Jesus' own brother, James, who had been a skeptic.

Thus, the inclusion of the gospel accounts further strengthens the case for the resurrection. It conforms with the proper tools of historiography, and the events in question are best explained by the hypothesis that Jesus was raised from the dead. Yet, the testimonies of the gospels are consistent with the proclamations of others.

The Testimony of the Early Church

As I pointed out in chapter six, 1 Corinthians 15:3-5b is considered to be in the form of a creedal statement. It is actually referred to as "The Creed of the Early Church." In that chapter, I demonstrated that this was likely in use by the community of Christians within only a few years of the events in question. This means that the testimony of the early church was that Jesus was executed, buried, and then raised from the dead in perfect symphony with what the gospels record.

The Testimonies of Skeptics

Surprisingly, all of the facts that I have laid out in this case are admitted by atheist and agnostic critics in modern scholarship. In chapter five, I recorded German atheist New Testament scholar, Gerd Ludemann, admitting the fatality of Jesus. That early believers had

---

[87]   Habermas, Gary & Licona, Michael, *The Case for the Resurrection of Jesus,* (Grand Rapids, MI: Kregel Press, 2004), 71.

what they thought were appearances of the risen Jesus is conceded by liberal, Jewish scholar, Paula Fredricksen. She explains,

> The disciples conviction that they had seen the Risen Christ, their permanent relocation to Jerusalem, their principled inclusion of Gentiles *as* Gentiles—all these are historical bedrock facts known past doubting about the earliest community after Jesus' death.[88]

The commitment level of the early church, that they were willing to die for their belief in the resurrection, was documented in chapter seven. Moreover, William Lane Craig affirms,

> One of the things that surprised me most in doing my doctoral work in Munich on the historicity of Jesus' resurrection was the dawning realization that most historical Jesus scholars who have written on the subject agree that (1) Jesus' burial by Joseph of Arimathea, (2) the discovery of Jesus' empty tomb by some of his female followers, (3) the post-mortem appearances of Jesus to various individuals and groups, and (4) the original disciples' coming sincerely to believe that God had raised Jesus from the dead despite their strong predisposition to the contrary are historical.[89]

Thus, modern scholars affirm "F., A., C.," and on the basis of this chapter "T.," of our case, but yet somehow deny the resurrection. It seems to me that if Jesus was dead, appeared later to others, and those

---

[88] Fredricksen, Paula, *Jesus of Nazareth*, (New York, NY: Vintage Books, 1999), 264.

[89] Craig, William Lane, "Contemporary Scholarship and Jesus Resurrection," (http://www.reasonablefaith.org/contemporary-scholarship-and-jesus-resurrection#ixzz2858nFaOa) Internet. Accessed 1 October, 2012.

others were so convinced of it that they were willing to die, then the resurrection is the only reasonable explanation.

The Testimony of the Believer

While this is not really an argument, I would say that those seeking to use apologetics for evangelistic purposes should be prepared to explain their own testimonies of what Christ has done in their own lives. Not only is this a practice in which Christians have always engaged, but it provides a compelling personal aspect to the truth of the resurrection. Such a powerful aspect of the believer's life should never be neglected.

Objections

CORE MOMENT

These objections can get kind of technical. If you're a beginner, it might be a good idea to just focus on the actual evidence we've covered so far. You can always come back to these objections once you've grown in your understanding a little more. If you think you're ready then keep reading. Just don't get discouraged if it's tough at first.

Don't extraordinary claims require extraordinary evidence?

As an actual avoidance of the arguments, some skeptics demand that the resurrection simply will not do as an explanation of the evidence merely because the claims are so outlandish. The belief in the resurrection is so extraordinary that it must require evidence that is similarly extraordinary. Such an objection sounds appealing but falls short of a refutation for several reasons. One problem with this kind of criticism is that it relies on a completely subjective new standard. Who is to say that an extraordinary claim requires extraordinary evidence? Worse still, who is to say what counts as an extraordinary claim? After all, for a theist, the claim of the resurrection is not nearly as extraordinary as it is for an atheist. If God exists as the creator of the entire space-time universe, then the idea that he could raise Jesus from the dead is entirely reasonable. Moreover, the bare-bones claim of the Christian apologist is that Jesus was dead for three days, then alive again. It is not extraordinary to claim that someone is dead. No one would see the claim that a person is alive as extraordinary either. What they find difficult to believe is how this state of affairs came about. Yet, if both of these simple claims can be demonstrated and defended, then it seems Christians have all the evidence they need to determine that Christ was raised, whether skeptics like this idea or not.

Transitioning the Presentation for the Layman

The *testimony* of man has now come into view. We can trust the testimonies recorded in the gospels because they pass the historical analysis mentioned above. I instruct students to ask those with whom they are witnessing why the gospels shouldn't be considered reliable in their historical assertions. Depending on how the individual responds, they can demonstrate that the gospel claims about the resurrection are multiply attested, admitted to by enemies of the faith like Paul, and contain facts that would be embarrassing to the authors. After this, I show them how to demonstrate that the early church had the same testimony.

It will be helpful for students to make some simple notes in their Bibles. At the top of the page containing 1 Corinthians 15, I instruct students to write "Galatians 1:18," so that they can easily locate the relevant biblical data. After doing this, students are prepared to explain that 1 Corinthians 15:3-5b is in the form of a creedal statement in use by the early church. Next, they can move to Galatians 1:18 and demonstrate that only three years after Paul's conversion he visited the church at Jerusalem and likely received the statement on that occasion. This means that almost immediately after the events surrounding the death of Jesus, people in Jerusalem were claiming that he had died, was buried and rose again. Thus, thinking people in the 21st century have powerful evidence that the testimony of these same individuals, who were willing to die for their message, believed exactly what we now claim.

Finally, I point out that even in the modern world, the testimony of the average citizen is that there is something special about Jesus. They find it hard to say critical things of him and point to him as an example for mankind. This places students in a position to seal the deal.

Conclusion

After studying this material, readers should understand that the testimonies of the gospels, the early church and modern believers are consistent. By demonstrating that the gospels are historically reliable regarding the events surrounding the crucifixion and resurrection, it becomes clear what the actual testimony of those writers was. Based on 1 Corinthians 15:3-5b, it is evident that the early church had a belief from the start that was consistent with the gospel story. Finally, by showing that modern man recognizes the remarkable impact that Jesus has had on history, and the incredible standard he provides for moral living, it is clear that the testimony of even today's unbelieving world is consistent with the message of the church. All of these facts can be explained to students in a fashion that is easy to remember. The most important thing, however, for *believers* to remember is that this is the point in the presentation when they should share their personal *Testimony* of faith.

Questions

1. Why does the "T." in C.O.R.E. F.A.C.T.S. stand for *Testimony*?
2. What is the testimony of the modern world about the person of Jesus?
3. Why can readers trust the gospels as historical material?
4. What is the testimony of skeptical scholars about "F., A., C., and T.?"
5. What was the testimony of the early church about Jesus?
6. What is the most important thing for *believers* to remember about "T.?"

$\mathcal{S}$

JESUS OFFERS SALVATION

For God so loved the world, that he gave his only begotten
son, that whoever believes in him shall not perish, but have
eternal life.—John 3:16

Introduction

The arguments have been made, the case has been set forth, the evidence has been revealed and the truth has been presented. After exploring these things it seems that the most reasonable move an individual can make is to surrender their life in commitment to the one true God as he has presented himself in Jesus. This short chapter will be my passionate invitation to unbelievers to make this most important decision. It will also be a clarion call for believers to share these C.O.R.E. F.A.C.T.S. with others.

What We Have Reason to Believe

A short summary of the case that is before us seems to be in order. During the first chapter it became clear that the evidence indicates that a being most adequately described as "God" must exist as the uncaused **Cause** of the natural universe. Next we learned that the universe is suspiciously well **Ordered** to permit life. Third, the moral argument demonstrates that if objective moral values and duties exist, then God must exist as a grounding for these **Rules**. On the basis of these arguments, it is reasonable to become open-minded to the prospect of having an immediate and personal *Experience* of God. The evidence shows that Jesus' wounds on the cross were, indeed, *Fatal*. It was then shown that he *Appeared* to various individuals after his death, alive and bodily. To firm up this truth, it was demonstrated that the disciples of Jesus had such a level of *Commitment* to this message that they were willing to die for it. The *Testimony* of the world, including skeptics, scholars, the early church, whole nations and modern man, is that Jesus was dead, buried and that others believed he had appeared to them. He is regarded as the most influential human being who has ever lived. On the basis of this, Jesus is also the way of *Salvation.*

CORE MOMENT

We have shown that there is a God and that he is revealed in Jesus. Based on the C.O.R.E. F.A.C.T.S., it seems logical to trust Jesus and commit to serving him.

Common Questions

Why should I make the commitment?

Despite the fact that his teachings are not politically correct, the divine Son of God should be regarded as the greatest purveyor of truth imaginable. He personally taught that he was the only way to experience God,[90] that in order to have this experience one must be born again,[91] and that apart from this, one will experience a very real separation from God called hell.[92] Naturally, there have been many who have committed their lives to the truth of the Christian message initially so that they could be "saved" from a future existence in

---

[90]   John 14:6

[91]   John 3:3

[92]   Luke 12:5, Mark 9:42-50, Matt. 10:28

hell. However, genuine believers quickly come to realize the joy of a relationship with God. This union is the greatest reason to embrace Jesus' sacrifice.

Why did Jesus need to die?

God's nature is one of justice. This cannot be changed anymore than a human can change the fact that he has a nature that is human. Thus, God must act justly. The problem is that when men and women commit sins they are sinning against an everlasting God. This means that the only just punishment for sin is an everlasting punishment. Unbelievers often criticize the faith because they feel that doctrines like this sound made up. However, all of us have an innate understanding of justice that bares this out.

Imagine the case of a man who kills his neighbor's pet cat. What is the just punishment for this. The man may have to pay a fine of some kind. Depending on where the event takes place, the penalty may be more serious. However, there is usually some kind of legal consequence for "sinning" against a cat, so to speak. Yet, what if the same man instead killed his human neighbor? There is a more hefty penalty for this. Based on the circumstances, he may be sent to prison for the rest of his life. He may end up receiving capital punishment. In other words, there is a much more serious legal consequence for "sinning" against another person. The reason for this is that we recognize a higher value for human life than we do for animal life. For most people, this seems to be the *just* response. The offender must pay for the crime of ending a life with much or all of his own life. Following this vein, imagine the just penalty for sinning against an everlasting God. If we continue to follow the innate sense of justice that led us to the understanding of the difference between "sinning" against an animal versus "sinning" against a man, then it should be clear that the penalty for sinning against God must be an everlasting penalty because of his everlasting nature. If God must act justly, because justice is a part of his nature, then he must allow sinners to receive this penalty in full.

The only way that such a penalty can be satisfied without condemning mankind to hell, is if an everlasting person could pay it for us. However, the only everlasting person capable of this is God himself. For this reason, God was loving enough to become a man himself and pay the penalty for the sin of human kind. Understood in this way, the atoning death of Jesus makes sense philosophically.

CORE MOMENT

Because God is just, he must punish sin justly. The just penalty for sinning against an everlasting God is an everlasting one. There is only one everlasting person. That person is God. So, God was the only One Who could pay the everlasting penalty for the sin of man.

What must I do?

It is not about doing something. The point of the message is what Jesus has done for you. However, Scripture explains that individuals who want to engage in a relationship with Jesus, and be sure of their salvation, will believe in Jesus, repent of their life of sin, and commit to live a life that testifies to this fact. It is appropriate to then follow the tradition and command of Jesus to be baptized as even he was and begin attending a group of likeminded believers in order that Christians can support each other and learn to become students of the Scriptures.[93] Moreover, those who accept this life will want to share the truth of this message with others. This is what it means to live the Christian life.

---

[93]   Matthew 28:19,20.

Transitioning the Presentation for the Layman

Hopefully, this will be one point in the method with which Christians are already familiar. Ultimately, all a trainer or facilitator needs to instruct a class to do is summarize the C.O.R.E. F.A.C.T.S. and invite the individual in question to take the reasonable step of committing their life to Jesus. A brief outline of steps students can take is in order.

— Invite the individual to make the commitment now or after consideration.
— Explain the need to repent of sin (repent means to turn from a life of sin).
— Point out that they need to confess their repentance and belief to others.
— Tell them that the first one they might confess this to is God himself.
— Instruct, or help them, to pray a prayer of commitment.

Conclusion

In this chapter it is made clear that the most reasonable response to the truth of the C.O.R.E. F.A.C.T.S. is to embrace the message of *Salvation*. There are many evangelistic strategies that could be employed at this juncture. What is supplied here is a simple way of confessing belief and committing to the Christian message. I have given an explanation of why the sacrifice of Jesus was necessary for the salvation of mankind and described the urgent need for men and women to embrace this offer. *Salvation* is the final, and most important truth of the C.O.R.E. F.A.C.T.S.

Questions

1. Why does the "S." in C.O.R.E. F.A.C.T.S. stand for *Salvation*?
2. Why should someone commit their life to Jesus?
3. Why was it necessary for Jesus to die as a sacrifice for sin?
4. What does the word *repent* mean?
5. What are some things a Christian might do after salvation?
6. How might one summarize the C.O.R.E. F.A.C.T.S.?

Appendix A

CONVERSATIONAL EVIDENCES FOR THE TRUTH OF CHRISTIAN THEISM

Introduction

In order to offer readers a more robust explanation of Christian defense, it is sometimes appropriate to discuss items other than those covered by the theistic and resurrection arguments. While those cases I believe are the strongest ones that can be made for the truth of Christianity, there are other facts about the nature of reality that tend to implicate the truth of the faith. Rather than attempting to put forth clinching philosophical arguments, some apologists will simply point out these facts about reality that may count as evidence for the truth of the Christian worldview. It would not be possible to cover all of the evidences that one could imagine. Nevertheless, what follows is a discussion of some of the types of facts used by these defenders so that readers can gain a sense of how to do a more conversational form of apologetics. Objections will not be given a great deal of consideration in this appendix. After all, these apologists do not necessarily maintain that their cases can be defended tooth and nail as do the proponents of other methods. The strength of the approach is not meant to be found in the defense of any individual evidence but in the weight of the totality of evidence.

A word should be said with regard to the difference between the terms "argument" and "evidence." As I use the term, an argument is a formal presentation of reasoning which leads to a valid conclusion. An evidence, however, may simply be a single piece of data that requires explanation. For example, the ORDER argument of chapter two includes two premises and a conclusion. However, the fact that human DNA is a highly complex blueprint of life, is a piece of evidence that needs to be explained. It is a piece of evidence that is often used in the ORDER argument, but is itself just a piece of data. C.O.R.E. F.A.C.T.S. apologists will setup their arguments and then begin mounting up evidence in support of each premise. In a conversational method apologists will, instead, mention the complexity and then point out that the complexity is best explained by a designer. It should be clear that there is a difference in formality between the two apologists, but they are aiming at the same target. If a conversational apologist makes a formal case in favor of his position, then he is using an argument. Conversely, if he is merely pointing out facts about the nature of reality, he is simply supplying evidence. It is, of course, usually true that what the conversational apologist is trying to say could be framed as an argument, but the real difference is in the methodology. Rather than formally making a case he is usually simply supplying evidence in a *conversational* way.

It is for this reason that I use the term *conversational* for this type of defense. The ideal setting for a conversational method, as far as I am concerned, is not on a platform in a formal debate. Rather, it is on a park bench, at a coffee shop, in the parking lot of a theater, or in homeroom. Whenever, and wherever facts are presented or stories are told, an apologist can point out how the subject at hand counts as evidence for the truth of the Christian message. As G.K. Chesterton wrote in *The Daily News*,

> You cannot evade the issue of God; whether you talk about pigs or the binomial theory, you are still talking about Him . . . . Things can be irrelevant to the proposition that Christianity is false, but nothing can be irrelevant to the proposition that Christianity is true. Zulus, gardening, butcher's shops, lunatic asylums, housemaids and the French Revolution—all these things not only may have

something to do with the Christian God, but must have
something to do with Him if He really lives and reigns.[94]

Thus, evidences often emerge in common places. It is because of
this that the methodology is flexible.

Evidences for God's Existence

Free will

One of the common evidences used in this approach is the
perceived reality of free will. By free will I mean the idea that man
has the actual ability to choose between two options. Typically,
what is being referred to is known as libertarian free will in which
an individual has freedom to make a non-determined choice. He
may be influenced by outside factors but not to the point of coercion.
This is, of course, the antithesis of determinism wherein all of man's
choices are determined by the chemistry of his body, his past personal
subjective experience, and little else. Between these two extremes lies
compatibilism. On compatibilism, man has freedom to do what he
wants, but has no control over his desires. His desires, however, are
what determine his actions. The term compatibilism is applied because
the idea is that the existence of man's free will is compatible with the
existence of some soft determinism over his desires. Nevertheless, it
would seem that the type of free will that the cumulative case apologist
is referring to is the commonly understood meaning of the term free
will. It is libertarian free will.

Most individuals will not find anything all that impressive about
the fact of free will, but this is precisely the point. Most people already
accept that they experience genuine freedom to make real choices.
What the apologist wants to say is that free will is best explained by
the existence of God. It may not seem immediately clear, why this is

---

[94]   Chesterton, G.K., (*The Daily News*, December, 1903).

the case, but at further investigation God's existence is the only live option. If naturalism is true, and by this I mean the natural universe is all that exists, then determinism is simply a fact of life. No one has the ability to make real choices, because whether or not they are aware of it, they are merely responding to the impulses, triggers and stimuli which have subtly nudged them toward each "decision." In the end, all events, whether caused by man or by the wind, are like a train of falling dominoes. No choice exists.

Conversely, if one is convinced that real choices do exist, then there must be a God who provided man with a special supernatural ability to make actual creative choices. The existence of free will is not as much something that is argued for by the conversational apologist as it is perceived. For this reason, the skeptic could conceivably deny that free will does exist. However, the apologist has set forth a piece of evidence for consideration that will be appealing to many.

Religious experience

Another piece of data that requires explanation is the fact that hundreds of millions of people throughout the history of the world have claimed to have experienced an obvious encounter with God. Whether in terms of a vision, prayerful communication or actual sensory contact, many humans seem to be absolutely convinced that God has connected with them in a real way. How can this be best explained? One might posit wish-fulfillment, delusion, the power of suggestion or a misinterpretation of the believer's conscious experience, but these would seem to be a stretch. The simplest and most obvious explanation is that many people have, indeed, had experiences of God.

In chapter four, I mentioned that this is not really a robust argument, but that makes it perfect as a piece of evidence for the conversational approach. If 99 people in a village claim to have met a particular man (*person Q*), and only one individual (*person S*) claims that *person Q* does not exist, which is the more likely to be true?

Should we believe that 99 villagers are wrong about the existence of *person Q*, or is it more reasonable to assume that *person S* is mistaken? *Person S* might demand that *person Q* does not exist because he has never seen him, heard his voice or met him at all. However, no thinking person would accept that *person S* is correct about *person Q* on the basis of this evidence. If 99 people claimed to have met *person Q*, and could tell powerful stories of experiences they have had with him, then it stands to reason that *person S* is merely overly skeptical.

Furthermore, of all the multitudes of people throughout human history who believed they had experienced God, if only one of them was correct, then he does exist. The same can be said of those who feel they have personally come to know Jesus Christ. Conversely, it is not true that if only one of them is wrong, then God does not exist. A similar analogy can make this point clearer. Instead of a village, let's consider the island of Nassau in the Bahamas.

Imagine a situation wherein many people claimed that Nassau did not exist. However, there were millions of people who claimed to have set foot on Nassau, but were mistaken. Maybe they had indeed been to other islands that they mistook for Nassau. One man, though, had indeed been to the actual island of Nassau and declared it to the world. He would be among the throngs who claimed to have walked the beaches of the place, but as long as he is indeed correct, then Nassau's existence is sure. Even if all other Nassau believers were wrong, his presence there would mean it was certain.

The evidence of religious experience is perhaps best explained by a theistic worldview. With the prominence of Christianity, it could be said that religious experience is best explained by biblical theism. After all, the three largest monotheistic religions are Judaism, Christianity and Islam. Jews and Christians claim to be serving the God of the Old Testament. This means that two of the world's three largest monotheisms claim the same God. In fact, Islam sees itself as coming after Judaism and Christianity. Though we would deny that our understanding of God is consistent with Islam's understanding of

Allah, Muslims claim to be worshipping the God of Abraham. Thus, all of the three largest monotheistic religions say they are focused on the God of the Old Testament. What I am not saying is that Islam is somehow true. Nor do I mean to say that I, in any sense, believe that Christians and Jews worship the same God that Muslims worship. What I am saying is that because the largest monotheistic religions in the world all point to the God of Abraham as their God, the vast majority of religious experiences claimed by monotheists are not just evidence for some generic philosopher's god but the God described by the Old Testament.

To be sure, there are criticisms that can be leveled against this explanation. On the surface, this strikes hearers as an example of the *ad populum* fallacy. That is to say, it sounds like the claim that something is true because many people adhere to it. It, like the other evidences in a conversational cumulative case approach, is just one piece of data that seems to lend favor to Christianity. There may be reasonable objections to this explanation of religious experience. For the advocate of this approach, however, it represents one more item that will help tip the scales in favor of the Christian worldview.

Consciousness

Current apologists, such as J.P. Moreland, have drafted formal arguments for God's existence on the basis of consciousness. However, for this approach, the human consciousness can be cited as an evidence in favor of the existence of the supernatural. As with the free will evidence, this issue is one that is perceived more than inferred. It seems obvious to most individuals that they have a subjective conscious experience of the world. This is an evidence against naturalism.

Most people are aware that they are not synonymous with their physical bodies. The way we talk and think about these earthen vessels demonstrates that we see ourselves as inhabiting but not being the same as them. If, for instance, we saw the human body as being synonymous with personhood, then an amputee would necessarily be less of a person. The same would be true of a physically smaller individual. Yet, we don't think of an infant as being less important, human or whole than an adult with larger stature or wider stance. Such would be ridiculous. However, if naturalism is true, then the human body *is* the person. What a man experiences as consciousness is merely the result of neurons firing in an intricate pattern. The truth of such a view would necessitate that we are little more than highly advanced computer software programs. There is no identifiable "self." There is only the machine. Average individuals will recognize this as surely false. Via perception, they simply know the truth. After all, if we were just highly advanced computers, then would we not lack consciousness? However, this does not explain why the existence of an intangible "self" would necessitate the falsity of naturalism.

Those who demand that there is an intangible self, are known as "substance dualists." They believe that man has both a physical body and an immaterial mind. Thus, he has two substances. Most models of substance dualism grant that the mind functions in the world via the physical body, but it is not synonymous with the material construct. If substance dualism is true, then it means that there is a supernatural "substance" of which the mind is a part. Because most individuals grant that they are not synonymous with their bodies, they unknowingly affirm substance dualism, including the existence of the supernatural realm.

Beauty

If God exists as the creator of the natural universe, then one might expect that the universe would be a basically beautiful one. While there are certainly features of the universe which one might rightly define as unattractive, ugly, or unpleasing to the senses, the overarching picture of the world is one that is intrinsically and amply ravishing. This amounts to a piece of data that requires explanation. If there were no God, then one might assume that the universe would be an unorganized, senselessly and unappealing conglomerate of material and color. Yet, as philosopher Richard Swinburne puts it,

> And finally, of course, God has reason to create a beautiful inanimate world—that is, a beautiful physical universe. Whatever God creates will be a good product; and so any universe he creates will be beautiful, as are humans and animals. Consider the stars and planets moving in orderly ways, and plants growing from seed into colorful flowers and reproducing themselves. Even if no one apart from God sees such a world, it is good that it exists.[95]

To put it a bit differently, if we had no sample universe from which to make a judgment call, it might be reasonable to imagine that a universe without a designer (as if such a thing were possible) would be a universe with only occasional and incidental beauty. Contrarily, we would imagine a designer would fill his universe with intentionally beautiful features. When one considers the absolute majesty of the actual universe, the most likely explanation is that there is a majestic artist by whom it was created.

Near-death experiences

Though there is much eye-rolling at the mention of this phenomena, the fact that many individuals have demonstrated what might rightly be called supernatural events at times in which their bodies were slipping off into death is worth considering. It is precisely the sort of evidence that fits within a conversational approach. Consider the data.

According to a 1982 Gallop poll ". . . five percent of the general population in the United States had undergone a near-death experience.

---

[95]   Swinburne, Richard, *The Existence of God,* (New York, NY: Oxford University Press, 2004), 121.

That was around eight million people then; now five percent is closer to fifteen million."[96] This alone should be reason enough to give such accounts a second look. One example is the research done in 1998 involving congenitally blind patients who were able to see for the first time during their near-death experience.[97] Just imagine. These individuals were born blind, but for the first time were able to describe the images of the world that seem so common to everyone else. Regarding the same study, Dinesh D'souza explains, ". . . They could give detailed descriptions of their medical procedures and even identify the jewelry and the colors of clothing of people around them."[98] This evidence is so hard to ignore because it was documented by professionals shortly after resuscitation, is not inconsistent and is testable. How were these individuals able to see if their physical eyesight was impaired? Could it be that they saw without the aid of their bodies because they were momentarily free of them?

Perhaps the most well-known work ever published on the subject of these experiences is the bestselling *Life after Life*[99] by Raymond Moody, MD. In it he lays out several commonalities of most near-death stories. Not every scenario contains all of these elements. Nevertheless they are the most regular:

- Ineffability, beyond the limits of any language to describe
- Hearing yourself pronounced dead
- Feelings of peace and quiet
- Hearing unusual noises
- Seeing a dark tunnel
- Finding yourself outside your body

---

[96] Atwater, P.M.H., *The Big Book of Near-Death Experiences*, (Charlottesville, VA: Hampton Roads Publishing, 2007), 9.

[97] Holden, Janice Miner & Greyson, Bruce, *The Handbook of Near-Death Experiences*, (Santa Brarbara, CA: Praeger, 2009), 120

[98] D'Souza, Dinesh. *Life after Death,* (New York, NY: Regnery Press, 2009), 64.

[99] Moody, Raymond. *Life After Life*, (San Francisco, CA: HarperOne, 2001).

- Meeting "spiritual beings"
- A very bright light experienced as a "being of light"
- A panoramic life review
- Sensing a border or limit to where you can go
- Coming back into your body
- Frustrating attempts to tell others about what happened to you
- Subtle "broadening and deepening" of your life afterward
- Elimination of fear of death
- Corroboration of events witnessed while out of your body
- A realm where all knowledge exists
- Cities of light[100]

The existence of the New Testament

The fact that the faith of the early church resulted in the production and collection of the books of the New Testament and that we have these documents in the 21st century is evidence that counts in favor of the reliability of those books. If these works were historically flawed, philosophically unsound, in indisputable conflict with each other or contained obviously fabricated stories, then they would have likely been discarded long ago. They have undergone serious scrutiny for centuries. Nevertheless, new generations of biblical scholars and historians are converted every decade.

The existence of the church

If the resurrection did not occur, then why is it that reasonable people devote their lives to the truth claims of Christianity? The central teaching of the church is the resurrection of Jesus. Absent of the resurrection, it makes no sense that educated individuals in the 21st century, let alone the 1st century, would have devoted their lives to

---

[100]   Atwater, P.M.H., *The Big Book of Near-Death Experiences*, (Charlottesville, VA: Hampton Roads Publishing, 2007), 10.

the church. This is similar to the argument from religious experience. However, this fact pushes the case beyond God's existence to the divinity of Jesus as Christ.

Transitioning the case for the layman

Little needs to be said in terms of how these evidences can be presented. Because the very nature of the case is conversational, it is also flexible in the way it is explained. With respect to the theistic and resurrection arguments, if one misses one of the key premises, or leaves out a relevant segment of the presentation, the whole argument might lose its potency. With this conversational approach, though, evidences to which an apologist might appeal, will differ based on the subject at hand, or the individual he wishes to evangelize. It is also important to remember that the evidences presented above represent only a sampling of possible elements one might use. Nevertheless, a short explanation of how this method can be employed will now be presented.

A facilitator might show a relevant segment from a piece of culture (film, television, music video, etc.), and then ask the group to point out aspects about the presentation that are best explained by Christian theism. If a character in a film is given a moment in which he must choose wisely or poorly, then the segment demonstrates the common belief in the existence of free will. This in turn points to the existence of God. In the event that a piece of culture points to the variety of world religions, students might point to the case from religious experience. A number of modern films explore the subject of artificial intelligence. This would be an excellent opportunity to discuss the evidence from consciousness.

A class of budding apologists could also be placed into groups and given scenarios in which they can improvise a conversational approach. "Group A" might be told that they have just heard a lecture on the migration of butterflies. "Group B" might be told that they heard a song that implies that love is merely about sexual gratification. "Group C" could be given the environment of a hospital waiting room where a family has just been told that one of their relatives has died. The role-playing Christian in "Group A" can talk about the beauty of the butterflies and the design of their migratory pattern. The one in "Group B" could discuss the fact that human beings are more than their physical bodies. "Group C's" Christian could talk about near-death experiences.

The possibilities are as plentiful as the subjects humans consider. Conversational approaches like this make for the simplest and most flexible ways to do apologetics. The setting is casual, the discussion does not require heated debate and the evidences do not need to be defended or argued to the hilt. It is for this reason that the approach is appealing to many.

Conclusion

Varying ways of teaching this method can be imagined by the facilitator, and numerous facts and truths can be incorporated. What is provided in this chapter is merely a snapshot of some of the pieces of data that may comprise a conversational approach to Christian apologetics. The method differs in very important ways from other methodologies in the field, but the goal is the same. Providing evangelicals with the means to incorporate apologetics into their evangelistic endeavors is vital, and the conversational method is yet another tool in the belt of the modern believer.

AN EASY REFERENCE OUTLINE
OF THE C.O.R.E. F.A.C.T.S.

CAUSE
— The universe had a <u>CAUSE</u>.
— Everything that begins to exist must have a <u>CAUSE</u> for its existence.
— The universe began to exist, therefore;
— The universe must have a <u>CAUSE</u> for its existence. The universe involves three things: TIME, SPACE and MATTER/ENERGY.
— Whatever <u>CAUSED</u> the universe must then be ETERNAL, SPACELESS and NON-MATERIAL. Nothing exists that meets these requirements and can do anything except "God."

ORDER
— The universe has <u>ORDER</u>.
— It either had to be that way, it happened by chance, or there is a designer.
— It didn't have to be that way, and it didn't happen by chance.
— There must have been a designer.

RULES
— The universe has <u>RULES</u>.
— If objective (real) moral <u>RULES</u> don't exist, then God doesn't exist.
— Objective <u>RULES</u> do exist, therefore;
— God exists.

EXPERIENCE
— People can have an immediate <u>EXPERIENCE</u> of God.

	— Every culture in history has believed EXPERIENCES of God happen.
	— You can EXPERIENCE God right now.
FATALITY	— The crucifixion of Jesus was FATAL.
	— Roman soldiers were expert killers.
	— Scholars agree that Jesus died on the cross.
APPEARED	— Jesus APPEARED to others after his death.
	— People were claiming he had APPEARED from the start.
	— Scholars admit that people thought Jesus had APPEARED to them.
COMMITTED	— The disciples were COMMITTED to the point of death.
	— People will live for a lie, but they will not die for a lie.
	— The disciples were willing to die for their belief in the resurrection.
	— They would have known if it was a lie.
TESTIMONY	— The TESTIMONY of man is that Jesus was raised.
	— Scholars agree on the facts about the resurrection mentioned above.
	— The gospel TESTIMONY is that Jesus was raised.
	— The TESTIMONY of the early church is that Jesus was raised.
SALVATION	— Jesus offers SALVATION.
	— Based on the C.O.R.E. F.A.C.T.S., God exists and Jesus was raised.
	— Jesus died for the sin of the world.
	— The most reasonable thing to do is accept Jesus right now.

APPENDIX C

A C.O.R.E. F.A.C.T.S. DEBATE

WHICH IS THE MORE REASONABLE POSITION, ATHEISM OR THEISM?

Introduction

In 2009, I had a debate with the administrator of a very successful atheist website. His name is Will. Subsequently we debated and chatted on my ministry's podcast and have always had spirited but friendly discussions of the evidence for the Christian faith. While I debated Harvard graduate, Daniel Alvarez, in 2010 before hundreds of onlookers, I thought the format and nature of this debate with Will was fitting to help readers better understand how to use the C.O.R.E. F.A.C.T.S. acrostic. There is an interesting story in this discussion. Will mentions in the debate that he is the son of a pastor and was raised in a Christian home. He and I have similar interests and even enjoy some of the same music. This made for a very exciting exchange.

It is important to remember that while this debate gets somewhat technical and involves some complicated issues, such is not usually the case when sharing the C.O.R.E. F.A.C.T.S. with friends and neighbors. Will is a well studied atheist who has made the research of these matters an important part of his life. Thus, I wouldn't want readers to get discouraged by the depth of this debate. I merely included it to show how well the C.O.R.E. F.A.C.T.S. stand up to heavy scrutiny.

BRAXTON'S OPENING REMARKS

BRAXTON: I want you to know what a privilege it is to be a part of this debate. And I appreciate my opponent for being willing to be involved. In all of my correspondence with him, he has been humble, kind and all the other things that I should be as a Christian, but so often fail. And I appreciate all of you who are following this debate and the interest you have in this important subject.

In this discussion, I am going to lay out what I believe to be the most compelling arguments for the existence of the theistic God. I am going to use an acrostic to help arrange my arguments so that it will be easier to remember. The acrostic I have created is C.O.R.E. F.A.C.T.S. In order to demonstrate that it is more reasonable to believe that God does not exist, my opponent will have to overcome each of the arguments and demonstrate why they are invalid. It should be noted from the start that these "C.O.R.E. F.A.C.T.S." are the arguments that best support my theistic worldview and so far in my discussions with skeptics and atheists I have yet to hear a compelling reason why these arguments are invalid.

The first of the C.O.R.E. F.A.C.T.S. that I will put forth is "**C.**"— *Caused*. The universe was caused. The argument has been classically known as the cosmological argument for the existence of God and it goes like this. 1) Everything that begins to exist had a cause for its existence, 2) the universe began to exist, thus 3) the universe had a cause.

Now this argument in and of itself may not seem to imply God, but at closer observation, I think you'll see that it does. Modern astrophysics have now confirmed beyond a reasonable doubt what theists have said all along. The universe was not always here. Since the early 90's physicists have had convincing evidence that the universe began to exist a finite time ago. When the background radiation wave still emanating from that explosion was discovered, astrophysicist George Smoot claimed, "If you're religious, it's like looking at God."

Why would he say such a thing? Modern science accepts the premise that the universe consists of at least three things: time, space and matter/energy. Whatever caused the universe to exist could not have been made up of these things or else it could not have caused their existence. This means, in brief, that whatever caused the universe to exist was not temporal, but eternal (non-temporal), not made of matter and does not occupy space. Confronted with this then impending evidence, agnostic astrophysicist Robert Jastrow claimed, "For the scientist who has lived by his faith in the power of reason, the story ends like a bad dream. He has scaled the mountains of ignorance; he is about to conquer the highest peak; as he pulls himself over the final rock, he is greeted by a band of theologians who have been sitting there for centuries."

In fact the argument is so strong that even without the evidence from modern cosmology, the universe had to come to exist for at least two reasons. 1) Time cannot extend infinitely into the past because if it did there would never have been enough time to arrive at today, and 2) we now know that the universe is expanding rapidly. If it is expanding, that means that if the tape could be rewound we would observe it retracting down to a single point and then nothingness.

This implies that an immaterial spaceless and timeless, intentional (because only an intentional being could have intended a universe) being caused the universe to come into existence.

"O." is the second core fact and it stands for *Order*. The universe exhibits incredible order. Stephen Hawking said in his book, *A Brief History of Time*, "It would be very difficult to explain why the universe should have begun in just this way, except as the act of a God who intended to create beings like us." Other scientists have said that it is like dozens of dials stand before us and if they were changed in the most infinitesimal way (if the gravitational force was slightly different or the strong nuclear force was changed or the electro-weak force) the universe would not be ordered as it is, but would result in chaos. This would seem to imply an intelligent designer.

"R." is for *Rules*. The universe seems to have guiding rules. These rules are not only the rules of mathematics and logic, but also the rules of morality. These rules are objective. 2 + 2 = 4. This is objectively true and will always be objectively true. The logical law of non-contradiction is objective. "A" can not be "A" and at the same time and in the same sense "non-A." In the same way, it is my contention that human beings have objective moral values. That is to say, it is wrong and it has always been wrong to torture innocent babies for fun. It is and always has been wrong to murder or rape. To maintain that these morals are not objective, but are subjective would be to say that there was nothing really wrong with the slaughter of six million Jews in the holocaust, or that pedophilia is not really wrong. These would just be preferences on atheism because there would be nothing really right or wrong at all. In fact we couldn't even speak of anything being better or worse than anything else. These terms are meaningless without objective moral values, and objective moral rules can only come from an objective moral rule-maker. I should also add that I am not saying that atheists cannot be moral. Indeed many atheists lead better lives morally than do many Christians. This is precisely the point. All men have the moral law written on their heart.

"E." is for *Experience*. Though I would not try to convince you of my own experience of God, without any compelling reasons to doubt these previous arguments, I see no reason to doubt my own experience of God. It is an experience that I would invite others to seek.

The F.A.C.T.S. arguments have to do with Jesus Christ. I think the best explanation for the events of the life of Jesus of Nazareth is that there is a God.

"F." is for *Fatal*. Jesus died by Roman crucifixion. This is accepted virtually across the board in modern scholarship. New Testament scholar, Gary Habermas, has counted the scholars for and against and shown that overwhelmingly Christ's death is affirmed among even skeptics in scholarship today. The idea that Jesus did not die is the modern day equivalent of the "flat earth theory."

"A." is for *Appearances*. Jesus appeared to many of his followers after his crucifixion. Though I will not use blind faith in the Bible, even the German scholar, Gerd Ludemann, (no friend to Christianity) affirms that what 1 Corinthians 15 says historically is true, namely that Jesus' followers had appearances of what they believed to be the risen Jesus. Moreover, there are creedal statements made there affirming Christ's resurrection that most scholars believe date back earlier than the documents themselves, placing them incredibly near the event itself. In other words, we have almost immediate evidence of individuals who saw what they believed to be the risen Christ. Even the hyper-skeptical *Jesus Seminar* affirms this truth.

"C." is for *Commitment level*. The commitment level of the early Christian church was so great, they were so convinced of what they saw, that they were willing to die for that belief. Men will live for a lie, but they will not die for something they know to be untrue. Muslim extremists may die for a lie, but they do not know it to be a lie. They believe. Many of these Christians would have known (if the resurrection were a fabrication) and died for a lie anyway.

"T." is for *Testimony*. This kind of commitment level developed because it was based on eye-witness testimony.

"S." is for *Salvation*.[101] The best solution to the question of what to do with these facts is surmise that Jesus really did die and rose again. As my friend, Mike Licona, says, "If a man claims to be God and rises from the dead we should believe him." If Jesus really did die and rose again, we have a divine miracle on our hands and that is evidence for the existence of God.

These are the C.O.R.E. F.A.C.T.S. of my position. If atheism is to be maintained, or for that matter agnosticism, then my opponent is going to have to respond to these arguments. Thank you.

---

[101] In the original debate I titled "S." *Solution*, because I had not yet settled on the final term "Salvation." however, I did not change the statements I made in support of that point. Thus, the comments of the debate are unaffected.

WILL'S FIRST CROSS-EXAMINATION

WILL: "C"—Can you demonstrate that the universe is not eternal, eternal both into the future and into the past? Can you demonstrate that if the universe had a beginning, there are no explanations but the Christian god?

BRAXTON: I would like to point out that I never claimed that the Christian God was the only possible designer based on the cosmological argument. That is a misunderstanding. The contention is that theism is more reasonable than atheism when cosmology is considered.

With regard to your question about the eternality of the universe, I contend that it is a logically indefensible position to hold that the universe has always existed. In order for this to be so, time would have to stretch eternally into the past. However, if time stretched eternally into the past, there would be an infinite number of points on that timeline stretching infinitely back. If there truly were an infinite number of points on that timeline, this point on that timeline that we are inhabiting now would have never arrived. This is why I said in my opening remarks that we would never have arrived at today.

WILL: "O."—Can you explain this quote from Hawking later in that very same chapter: "But if the universe is really completely self-contained, having no boundary or edge, it would have neither beginning nor end: it would simply be. What place, then, for a creator?" Why does order imply an intelligent designer? Can you demonstrate that order cannot be without an intelligent designer?

BRAXTON: Stephen Hawking is a theoretical physicist. Thus, what he says about what the furniture (and form) of the universe might look like is to be taken as hypothetical. I mentioned him because he sees that if the universe has a beginning then it implies God. However, science is not in his corner on the hypothesis that the universe has no beginning or end. The simple philosophical demonstration I just mentioned above shows that there are no actual infinites in the universe. Moreover, Penzias and Wilson discovered the cosmic background radiation which demonstrates that the universe is in a state of expansion. If it is expanding then its expansion had to begin.

Concerning the question of why order implies intelligence, I would first say that the burden of proof would fall on the side of naturalism to demonstrate an example of random variation resulting in anything remotely like the level of complexity we observe in the universe. Bill Gates claimed, "DNA is like a computer program, but far, far more advanced than any software we've ever created." Beyond that I would remind you of the points I made in my opening remarks.

WILL: "R."—Can you demonstrate that morality is objective and predates the development of life on earth, as opposed to a system of behaviors that developed slowly as species became more social and morality and ethics became a necessary part of survival?

BRAXTON: With regard to the moral argument I set forth, I do think that we can demonstrate that an objective moral code does exist and not only would I contend that it was an objective reality before mankind, but I would further say that it would be an objective reality even if man had never existed in the universe. Arguments such as Richard Dawkins' selfish gene construct do not explain the moral actions taken by some which lend no help to their own situation or that of their offspring. For example, the Amish community that forgave and made food for the murderer of two of their girls; this would not be explained by the idea of moral evolution. Moreover, as I said before, nothing would really be *wrong*. If a man decided it was moral for him to go about raping young girls, no one could tell him that he was morally wrong for doing so. It would merely be his preference. But, I think morality is objective and deep down I think we all know it.

WILL: "E."—Have you ever taken any mind-altering drugs?

BRAXTON: To clear the record, I have not ever taken any mind altering drugs and if Will has, I trust that he will inform me of any theological value found therein.

WILL: "F." Can you cite non-biblical references from the time Jesus was supposedly alive, specifically detailing his death?

BRAXTON: I am prepared to produce extra-biblical evidence for the death of Jesus by crucifixion. Cornelius Tacitus lived from 55 A.D. to about 120 A.D. and he claimed, "Consequently, to get rid of the report, Nero fastened the guilt and inflicted the most exquisite tortures on a class hated for their abominations, called Christians by the populace. Christus, from whom the name had its origin, suffered the extreme penalty during the reign of Tiberius at the hands of one of our procurators, Pontius Pilatus . . ." Pliny the Younger and Thallus also gave testimony to his death. This kind of testimony is almost unheard of in ancient historiography. Because of this, eminent atheist New Testament scholar Gerd Ludemann, states, "Jesus' death as a consequence of crucifixion is indisputable." Fellow of the hyper-skeptical Jesus Seminar, John Dominic Crossan, admits, "That [Jesus] was crucified is as sure as anything historical can ever be."

WILL: "A."—Can you cite non-biblical references from the time of the disciples that confirm the appearance of Jesus and that rule out any other explanation?

BRAXTON: I can produce first century confirmation of the appearances (Clement's letter to the Corinthian church, for example); however, if what you are looking for is non-Christian first century confirmation, a note should be made. To ask for non-Christian eyewitness testimony of the risen Christ would be tantamount to asking for an eyewitness to a car wreck who doesn't believe the car wreck happened. You asked if I could produce testimony that would rule out any other possibility. I would say that the resurrection is the only explanation that is not inconsistent, has vast explanatory scope and great explanatory power. Produce another alternative that you feel meets the requirements and I will deal with it. It should be stated that virtually no one, Christian or otherwise, in scholarship denies that the followers of Christ experienced what they viewed to be appearances of the risen Jesus.

WILL: "C." Can you demonstrate that the commitment level of the early Christian church is greater than every other known religion?

BRAXTON: Your question of whether I could demonstrate that the commitment level of the early church was greater than that of any other religion is a misunderstanding of the argument. That is not what I am claiming. In fact I can imagine no greater commitment level than that of those who die in an act of Jihad. My contention is that their commitment level was such that they were willing to die for something that (if it was a fabrication) they would have *known* to be untrue. Of course the faithful of many religions have died for things that are untrue. The difference is that many first century Christians died for something that (if it were fabricated) they would have known to be false.

WILL: "T."—Are people capable of lying, exaggerating, embellishing, or remembering incorrectly?

BRAXTON: The simple answer is "of course." But I would not die for something I fabricated. The problem with this sort of argument is that it doesn't explain the level of persecution that the early church endured.

WILL'S OPENING REMARKS

I used to be a Christian. I was born in a Christian home, went to church, watched my dad become a pastor, went on to teach Sunday School and eventually adult Bible classes in church. The single most important part of religious experience, I was taught, was faith. You have faith in god, you have faith that Jesus died for your sins, and you have faith that you're going to heaven for believing. Never were we asked to demonstrate the existence of god scientifically because that would mean that we didn't have faith. Faith had to happen without proof or it ceased to be faith. After leaving religion, I thought about this a great deal. What was faith? Why was it such an important part of Christianity, and as I studied more a part of Judaism, Islam, Hinduism, and any other theistic faith I could study? It didn't really occur to me until I had my first religious debate of this kind. I had a discussion (argument) with a friend of mine about the Shroud of Turin. He insisted that it was evidence of Jesus and I had no idea why he was looking for evidence. Why would you need evidence when you have faith? Then it dawned on me. The reason he needed evidence was doubt. Just like me, faith wasn't enough for him. He had to try and rationalize and explain everything with evidence and science and whatnot. I felt badly telling him that the Shroud was a fake, but I didn't want to lie to him. Doubt is what happens when faith fails, and because many human beings are often curious and skeptical by nature, doubt has the tendency to enter even the most devout and pious believer's mind.

People don't believe in god because someone presents them with a very solid piece of verifiable evidence. That just doesn't happen. If such compelling evidence existed, you can bet that people like me, skeptics, would love to get my hands on it so I can test and verify it. No, people believe in god either because they're born into it, or because they're "born again," in that the church provides something for them, be it community, emotional support in a time of need, etc.

When a skeptic like me is presented with supposed evidence for god, it's generally not difficult for me to systematically dismantle it not because I'm smarter or anything like that, but because religion requires faith. The supernatural requires faith. Now, I don't really have a problem with faith unless it makes people do harmful things, but faith isn't supposed to be rational or logical or scientific. It's something completely different. Show me a person that decides that the earth is 6,000 years old and he or she needs to invent a bunch of bonk science to back it up and I'll show you someone that's trying to deal with doubt.

With all respect, I've seen all of your arguments before, and many, many more. As a moderator of an atheist forum, I suppose I've put myself in a position to be exposed to a lot of people that want to convince me of god's existence using my own rules, rules of science and logic, instead of their rules, rules of faith. It's not that they're not capable of logic and scientific understanding, it's just that they're able to turn it off when it comes to the supernatural because it's worth it to them. But honestly, unless there's an entirely new argument or piece of evidence, I already know what you're going to say as I've responded to it many times with a very high rate of success.

God is contradictory.

Let's look at a very basic construct of god common to most religions:

— God is not evil, but in fact benevolent
— God understands what evil (I'm using "evil" loosely here) is and that it exists
— God is omnipotent
— God intervenes, or somehow is active in his creation

Assuming these axioms, one (like Epicurus) must conclude that one of these things is wrong.

Is god willing to prevent evil, but unable? If so, he is not omnipotent.

Is god able to prevent evil, but not willing? If so, he is not benevolent.

Is god both willing and able to prevent evil? This cannot be as there is evil.

Is god neither able, nor willing? If so, he is not god.

I would be uncomfortable having an understanding of the universe which is inherently contradictory. Science, math, logic, they all follow definite rules and those rules are eventually knowable and you can even make predictions based on those rules. If, however, there were contradictions in science, math, or logic, they would fail to be useful to me in understanding reality.

There are better explanations as to the roots of theism. I'd like you to imagine yourself living in Northern Africa about 20,000 years ago. You're a member of a roving tribe of hunter-gatherers. Life is relatively simple: you wake, eat, hunt, eat, then sleep. On a bad day, you have to fight off a predator or deal with harsh weather. On a good day, you have extra food from before or mate. You're able to do so well, better than other competing species, because you're able to understand other members of your tribe. You may not have a fully formed language yet, but through various gestures and noises, you can communicate, and you're able to understand them because they developed similar abilities. Commonality (the ability to understand what they are thinking and postulate what they are trying to communicate) has given you a huge survival advantage.

The process of your species' development means that you have a natural curiosity. The same curiosity that your ancestors used to develop the first tools, shovels, clothing, and hunting weapons. The curiosity has grown as members of the species with more curiosity have been able to develop better technologies for survival and have had the opportunity to mate more, passing along that trait. You're the culmination of many, many generations of curious people. You were curious about how the short-nosed bear was able to access bone marrow in a kill, so you used a heavy stone and a strong stone as hammer and chisel to crack the thick bone of a bison. The nutrient-rich marrow helps to feed you and your tribe, and they now have a new technique for extracting more from each kill. High-five.

One day you're feeling particularly curious about the sun. What is the sun? It brings light, heat, better fruits and vegetables and means that there will be more prey to be caught. It's pretty darn special, you reckon. But how do you understand the sun? You don't have thousands of years of scientific discovery to tell you that it's the mass of incandescent gas at the center of our solar system, so you're left with what you understand. You understand basic communication, personal relationships and sympathy. So you test it. One day, you try a ritual of some kind, and the next day happens to be warm. Or cold. Or anything, really. You take that to be a direct result of what you've done, and religion is born. Soon you're not as much a hunter as you are a shaman or priest, interpreting signs from the sun and teaching other members of your tribe what pleases the sun.

When we look back to the very first religions in recorded history, they're mostly polytheistic and naturalistic, or worshiping natural phenomena. Even today, when we encounter lost tribes that have never come into contact with civilization, they generally have naturalistic religious practices and beliefs. Notice that in my hypothetical I did not violate any laws of science or logic. All of what I described could very well have happened without any divine intervention or supernatural occurrence.

The alternative is incredibly complex and requires the supernatural. Before time began there was a creature which has always existed with limitless power and the ability to know everything. One day (actually not one day, as time didn't exist yet) this being decided to create reality. Depending on the religion, he/she/it created the universe with the world in it. No existing religious texts describe the universe beginning the way scientists believe (boom, matter, gravity collecting matter into discs, inner discs igniting and outer discs turning into asteroid fields and planets, some planets happening to be solid instead of mostly gas, some of those planets have the right combinations of things to eventually have liquid water, abiogenesis, evolution of single celled aquatic organisms, multicellular aquatic life, complex aquatic life, simple land plants, complex land plants, complex land animals, etc.), so there was even more supernatural stuff going on. In Judaism, Christianity and Islam, it's heavens and the earth, light, expanse between waters, oceans and land, vegetation, day and night, water creatures, birds, land creatures, and humans. Not exactly the order scientists have rested on.

So let's say that you take two average people born without religion (as people aren't born knowing religion). You take each of them aside and the first person is told the story about the hunter-gatherer worshiping the sun, the second person is told that god is real. How do you think that would turn out?

BRAXTON'S FIRST CROSS-EXAMINATION

BRAXTON: First, I would like to know what kind of evidence it would take in order for you to be convinced that theism is true.

WILL: The problem is that one cannot demonstrate the supernatural naturally. Let's say that god appears in front of me and I ask him to prove his power. "God," I'd ask, "please demonstrate your power by doing something which cannot be explained." He does something like making the earth suddenly rotate in the opposite direction, which I then begin to investigate. How would I investigate this? Modern science cannot explain this, but what if there is a perfectly reasonable explanation? What if this god is an impostor, an individual from an intelligent and more technologically advanced race of beings that can easily reverse the rotation of the planet? Because that explanation may not violate the laws of physics, it's actually more likely than the god hypothesis.

I suppose the answer is "Such evidence likely does not exist, so I can't predict what it would look like."

BRAXTON: What is your understanding or definition of the term "faith" with regard to Christianity? On what basis have you established that understanding or definition?

WILL: Education in the church was the source of my understanding of faith. People have faith in god, they don't investigate god carefully in a laboratory and come to a verifiable conclusion.

BRAXTON: You claimed, "I've put myself in a position to be exposed to a lot of people that want to convince me of god's existence using my own rules, rules of science and logic, instead of their rules, rules of faith." On what basis do you claim that the rules of science and logic are only available to skeptics and atheists?

WILL: Those same rules are available to everyone, but they don't always apply to everything. 99.9% of the time, I'm sure you are just as capable as I to utilize science, logic, deductive reasoning, etc. in your everyday life to help you through, but when it comes to religion, requiring verifiable scientific evidence doesn't work. You are welcome to look back at the archives of our forum to see all of the theists that have brought forth arguments like the god of the gaps, cosmological fallacy, etc. In every one of those cases without exception, there has been either a mistake or assumption which can be found, exposed, and then corrected for.

BRAXTON: Is it your contention that the premises that you set forth in your opening remarks, regarding the problem of evil, are the only possibilities available to us?

WILL: The best argument I've ever heard in response to the Epicurean god-paradox is regarding free will, but even that doesn't negate the argument. The facts are still there and they are still contradictory.

BRAXTON: You claimed, "No, people believe in god either because they're born into it, or because they're 'born again,' in that the church provides something for them, be it community, emotional support in a time of need, etc." Can you demonstrate that this is a universal norm, or is it merely conjecture?

WILL: I can demonstrate that most people are religious because they're born into it. That can be verified by the fact that if you are born into a Christian home, there's a very, very high probability that you will be Christian for the rest of your life. If you're born into a Muslim home, there's a very, very high probability that you will be Muslim for the rest of your life. This applies to all religions. No statistics are available as to the most common reason for born-again believers to join their new religion, so I suppose that would be conjecture. Unfortunately, the only information we can draw on is personal experience.

WILL'S FIRST REBUTTAL

"C" — 1 Everything that begins to exist had a cause for its existence
2 the universe (actually all of reality) began to exist
3 [therefore,] the universe had a cause

What does this argument have to do with god? Nothing in this suggests a Judeo-Christian or Muslim god, nothing in it suggests a Pagan god, nothing in it suggests even any kind of god. It could just as easily be something which we cannot possibly understand in any way. This could just as easily demonstrate a new scientific phenomena. The bottom line is we don't know what caused the Big Bang. Scientists are still working on it, so we don't have an answer yet. Still, that answer being unknown does not automatically fall back to "god did it."

This is what we call a "god of the gaps" argument. If something is unexplainable by science, it must therefore be attributed to god. I cannot explain why American Idol is popular, therefore it is evidence of god. I cannot explain quantum superposition, therefore it's evidence of god. Obviously, these are not logically defendable conclusions, as the logic is fallacious.

"O."—I'm going to tackle the ordered part of this instead of your suggestion that Stephen Hawking is a theist.

You didn't really go into detail on this one, so I'm going to assume you're making the fine-tuned universe argument, which I'm afraid is flawed. The universe is ideal for life because life has evolved within the laws of nature. Any life form which formed for different laws would die out and not continue on. Whatever the laws of nature might be, they are necessarily ideal for anything existing within that reality.

Let's say that the earth didn't revolve around an average star, but a red giant. Abiogenesis occurs and life begins to evolve. Instead of the mutations that work best with an average star, the mutations that work best with the red giant survive, and life continues to evolve according to the reality in which it exists. Let's say that gravity is stronger so stars form more quickly and burn faster, and planets revolve at a greater distance and faster. Still, any life that happened on these worlds would have mutations, and any mutations that fit with higher gravity would mean better survival.

The universe isn't ordered for us, we've adapted to the universe. For proof of that, all you need to know is that 98% of all species to develop on earth have died out.

"R."—The arbitrary lawgiver? No, I'm afraid there's a simple explanation for human morals, and it lies, like the answer above, in evolution. This is one of my favorite answers because I love evolutionary sociology.

I'm going to assume you understand the principles of evolution. So let's say that you're back 20,000 years ago again. Life is a struggle for survival and adaptation. Humans that cared for their children were more likely to have their genes passed on to the next generation, so that trait became strong. Humans that cared for their kin also were more likely to have their genes passed on to the next generation, so that trait became strong. Mating for humans requires cooperation in order to stand the best chance at success, so humans which could cooperate with and feel attached to our mates were more likely to have their genes survive. Finally, as a social species, cooperation within the tribe, band or what have you meant a better chance at survival. The cost of having to split resources was outweighed by the benefit of cooperating for hunting, protection and gathering, so the humans that were best at cooperating within a basic social structure would be more likely to survive and pass on genes.

Morality's genesis was in evolutionary survival, not in being handed down from a creator. Killing many people is damaging to the species, so it is immoral. Raping a child damages the next generation and is thus damaging to the species. Rape contradicted what I explained above about mating and cooperation.

Unfortunately, these moral realities are often ignored in religious texts, such as the Torah/Bible. Beating children is endorsed in Proverbs 13:24. Murdering people is constantly in the Bible (Deuteronomy 17:12, Leviticus 20:13, Leviticus 20:27, Exodus 21:15, and my favorite 2 Chronicles 15:12-13). Rape is ordered by the God of the Bible in Judges 21:10-24 (and a few more times in Deuteronomy). Indeed, there is even genocide ordered by God in the Bible (Leviticus 26:7-9). I can list similar verses from the Qur'an. It is my contention that one cannot attribute the source of morality to a character which is immoral.

"E."—I see no reason that you should doubt the experience of a Muslim that has experienced the presence of Allah, or an ancient Greek that experienced the presence of Apollo. Their experiences are no less or more real than your own experience. If I told you that I died and experienced no heaven, you would doubt my experience?

"F."—I'd really like to see citations for this, because I've already verified many times that this isn't true. There is no extra-Biblical evidence of the existence of Jesus, which is peculiar because historical records from Palestine around 2000 years ago are quite well documented. The first historical records of Jesus (the Gospels) are from early Christians around 70AD, which is at least 40 years after the supposed ascension, and well after the deaths of any disciples or really anyone that knew Jesus as the life expectancy back then was about 30-35 years. In other words, there are no existing first-hand accounts of Jesus in existence.

"A."—How many people claim to have seen Bigfoot first hand? How many people report having been abducted and sexually assaulted by aliens? Do you believe in the existence of something simply because someone has reported to have experienced it? Would you believe me if I told you that when I was on a commercial flight from Dallas/Ft. Worth to SFO I saw a Pegasus flying outside my window?

"C."—People of all religions and all politics die for their beliefs. It does not make them any truer, in fact it communicates obsession.

"T."—Same as above. Pegasus?

"**S.**"—I had heart surgery when I was 5 years old. Part of the process meant having my heart stop beating for about 15 seconds, leaving me very much dead. If I had claimed to be god before going in to surgery, would I be god?

BRAXTON'S SECOND CROSS-EXAMINATION

(Note to observers: During cross examinations I'm not presenting or defending my arguments. I will do that in rebuttal.)

BRAXTON: Is it your assumption that the *Ordered* (fine tuning) argument is aimed exclusively at the improbability of the development of biological organisms? How do you explain the incredible degree of fine tuning found throughout the universe, aside from life forms?

WILL: One cannot demonstrate that the universe is fine tuned unless it can be determined what the likelihood is that the universe could be another way. Certainly we can imagine in what ways the universe could be different, but without understanding basically everything about the history of our universe, there's no way we could say, "Ah, but there's a 25% chance it could have happened like this . . ." Basically, no such fine-tuning can be demonstrated at all, regardless of what the unnamed scientists you were citing claimed. In fact, Stephen Hawking himself on page 124 of *A Brief History of Time* basically endorses what's called the "weak anthropic principle," or the idea that if conditions weren't right for humans as they are, sure humans wouldn't exist, but we can't speak to the likelihood of our particular universe.

BRAXTON: Is it your view that there are no objective moral values?

WILL: Not from religion, no. One could argue that the moral code which developed as humans developed socially is objective, but I think that would be an unfair stretching of the word "objective." At best we have a collective of subjective morals. Objective morals would suggest an outside and supreme player to judge, and you can't assume god when you're making the case for his/her/its existence.

BRAXTON: Can you demonstrate that the life expectancy in the Near East during the first century was only 30-35 years? If so, can you demonstrate that it is highly unlikely that any of Jesus' contemporaries lived to at least 70 A.D.?

WILL: [Here, Will provided some data that demonstrated that many individuals died as infants, but it also showed that for those who survived childhood, 70 or more years was an average lifespan]

The problem with your second question is that I was referencing a specific piece of evidence which is attributed to a specific author (though we're not 100% sure about that one because it wasn't attributed until 150A.D.), Mark the Evangelist. According to our best understanding, Mark was a traveling companion of Paul and never met Jesus, though he may have been alive before the supposed time of Jesus' ascension. It's widely assumed that Mark got his information orally from Peter.

BRAXTON: Can you point me to a documented account of any instance wherein a group of individuals experienced an alien abduction (or the equivalent) and were so convinced that they were willing to die for the veracity of such a claim?

WILL: They wouldn't need to die for the veracity of their claim, so it's not the same thing.

BRAXTON'S FIRST REBUTTAL

It is important to note that you respectfully criticized my arguments because you have heard them before and others have already engaged them. This seems hardly fair since you subsequently used the "Problem of Evil" argument which is literally ancient and has been engaged many more times and by many more philosophers than any of mine.

You claim that I am arguing for the "god of the gaps," but this is a misunderstanding of the cosmological argument ("C."). Respectfully, this may be why many atheists continue to argue poorly against this argument. In order for this to be a "god of the gaps" argument, it would require that we have no evidence for the cause of the universe and so we assume God. On the contrary, I stated before that the cause of something cannot be the something that is caused. Thus, since the universe is made up of time, space and matter, it is necessary that whatever caused those things to come into existence is not made up of them. This means that far from no evidence, we have positive evidence that whatever caused the universe to exist was eternal, spaceless, not material and intentional in that it had to intend to create. It would have to be all powerful to create the universe out of nothing and these attributes are enough to justify that theism is more reasonable than atheism.

You never responded to my argument that an infinite regress is not possible. Rather, we heard an argument for the infinite universe. Steven Weinberg and Hawking himself admit that it is outdated. In fact, Hawking claimed of the background wave radiation that it was "the final nail in the coffin of the steady state." By the way, I did not claim in my argument that Hawking was a theist. It is common in debate to use the very words of your opponents. My point was that Hawking admitted that if the universe was not infinite it would be hard to surmise anything other than a creator.

You claim that the universe is not fine tuned because we cannot demonstrate that it could have happened any other way. 1) If we were in a room with a beautiful painting we would never have had to see another beautiful painting to surmise that the painting had been painted. 2) There are literally infinite numbers of other possibilities, and 3) The greatest probability is that the universe would never have come to exist at all on its own because out of nothing, nothing comes!

I appreciate your honesty in admitting that moral values are not objective without God, but I wonder if everyone observing really understands the implications of this. This would mean that if another dictator, such as Adolf Hitler, were to come to power and his ideology became the norm, so that it was considered good for mankind to kill Jews in horribly torturous ways, then there would be nothing really wrong with that. It would also mean that if an alien race came to earth and had a different morality that said treating humans like cattle was the way to go, then this would not be wrong either. These would just be preferences. Are we really willing to say that? By the way, I am not arguing for this position based on what others have done, but it is interesting to note that Francis Collins, who headed up the "Human Genome Project," not only became a theist, but a Christian theist because he became convinced of objective morality. He would be well aware of what the influence of evolution would be on this matter.

You claim to have verified that the majority of scholarship does not affirm the historical reality of the man, Jesus. However, you may feel this way, but this is highly unlikely since you would have had to have counted them. This is a process that takes years, even longer if you don't have access to major online paid databases. Gary Habermas has counted. He lays out the data in his book, *The Historical Jesus*, and describes the process on his website. Moreover, I have cited some of the most skeptical scholarship out there, naming Gerd Ludemann and The Jesus Seminar. Moreover, Bob Price does deny the historical Jesus, but at least he admits that he is on the fringe of scholarship.—See his debate with Habermas and Licona on the Infidel Guy radio show.

Not only did I provide you with first century extra-biblical evidence for the historical Jesus, but the evidence you cited for the life expectancy of first century individuals actually confirms my position and refutes yours in that it shows that if an individual survived infancy, they had a fair chance of living beyond what we would consider "midlife" by today's standards. Besides, Tacitus lived to be 61, and Josephus lived to be 60, just to name a couple.

You claim that people of all persuasions died for their beliefs. Fine, I did not contest that. I argued that these individuals [Christ's disciples] would have died for something they knew to be untrue [if it had indeed been fabricated]. I have already cited evidence for the appearances from skeptical scholarship. This is why skeptics like Bart Ehrman try to explain the appearances based on delusion or group hallucination.

You claim that you died and came back to life. You had a near-death experience, not a death experience. However, if you really believe that you died, brain cells and all, and rose again, then I don't know why you have a problem with the resurrection.

You seem to have a poor understanding of what the term "faith" means within Christianity, which is understandable because many Christians do too. But orthodox Christianity has never held that faith means blindly accepting something without any evidence at all. On the contrary, Christianity has historically maintained that its adherents have trust (faith) in what God will do in the future based on what we can demonstrate happened in the past. Such an idea as you described is known as "fideism" and has been rejected by even the Roman Catholic church.

As far as presenting arguments for the reasonability of atheism, you have really only used the well known "Problem of Evil" argument, alongside what has come to be known as the "Atrocities of the Old Testament." The problem with the "Problem of Evil," is that it commits the fallacy of the "faulty dilemma." Basically, it assumes that God would have no basis for allowing evil, if he is a good God, thus God cannot exist. However, there may be good reason to allow evil in the world. And it is certainly not a problem unless one both believes in God and is at the same time a mortalist, which is unlikely.

As far as the "Atrocities of the Old Testament," this is not a debate regarding bibliology or biblical inerrancy. While I personally think there are answers to all the passages you brought out, even if you were able to show that these are inconsistent with the nature of God, it would only affect those Scriptures and not God's existence. Once again, although I have my own views I am not arguing for biblical inerrancy here.

You used a hypothetical explanation of how religion forms. However, even if this is true of how some religions have come to be (and I'm sure it is), it is a leap in logic to assume that it is how all religions form. Moreover, you have committed the "genetic fallacy" which is an attempt to discredit one's belief based on how they arrived at that belief.

You also argued that most people are a part of the religion they are a part of because they were born into that religion. Once again this commits the "genetic fallacy."

You claim that people don't come to faith because they examined the evidence and arrived at the conclusion of Christianity. This is simply not true. I know many people who have arrived at Christianity through an examination of the evidence. Besides, I don't see how you could demonstrate such a claim.

Finally, you admitted that there is no evidence you can imagine that would convince you of theism because any natural explanation would be better than a supernatural one. This is a presuppositional embrace of naturalism and indicates that one is willing to follow the evidence as long as it does not affect his own prior commitment. It is what philosophers call theoretical accommodation. David Hume held the same view and has been discredited for it. Anthony Flew spent his life defending atheism, but recently embraced deism because he rejected this *a priori* assertion against the supernatural and rather followed the motto "follow the evidence wherever it may lead."

WILL'S SECOND CROSS-EXAMINATION

WILL: Do you think that the age of an argument is relevant in determining whether it is correct or incorrect?

BRAXTON: No, I do not think the age of an argument really matters. I responded to your Epicurus argument. The reason I mentioned its age and the overwhelming attention that has been given to it is precisely because you criticized my C.O.R.E. F.A.C.T.S. argument since it is comprised of arguments that are familiar.

WILL: What in the cosmological argument specifically leads one to theism? Why are any and all scientific hypothesis regarding the beginning of existence dismissed, instead replaced specifically by the concept of god? Is this not the very definition of the "god of the gaps" fallacy?

BRAXTON: The Kalam (impossibility of an infinite regress) aspect of my cosmological argument invalidates all other known cosmological explanations. Kalam alone would be a "god of the gaps" argument, but not when the necessary definitions of the first cause I mentioned previously are considered.

WILL: Hawking has said that the current incarnation of the universe is not infinite, but what has Professor Hawking said about the Cyclical model?

BRAXTON: Hawking's cyclical model (or any other of the many cyclical models) still does not solve the problem of the impossibility of an infinite regress so long as there are points (events, or points in time) on the timeline. The reason for this is that if there are points then there must be a first point.

WILL: How can one compare a painting, something we know to be created, with the universe, something we are debating whether or not was created? Moreover, if we were in a room with a painting and had no knowledge of any other rooms to compare our room to, is it possible (or rather not completely impossible) that the painting could have another explanation?

BRAXTON: My contention is that even if we had never seen a painting it would be evident that the painting had been created because of specified complexity. You may be used to seeing this argument posed against evolution, but Darwinism is helpless here because there is no mechanism. I'm not sure I follow your second question, but if I understand what you're asking then I would say, "No."

WILL: Is it possible you missed my discussion about how morality developed from evolution and that things like murder, rape, etc. are considered innately wrong because of said evolution? And are you aware that many scientists are concerned about Francis Collins' religiosity?

BRAXTON: I did not miss your argument from sociological evolution, and I'm quite sure it does bother *some* other scientists that Collins disagrees with them.

WILL: Have you read "Review of Habermas" by Peter Kirby, which demonstrates numerous mistakes on the part of Christian apologist Gary Habermas?

BRAXTON: I read the electronic document by that title. Unfortunately, I saw nowhere that Kirby specifically addressed the opinion of the majority of scholarship argument that I brought up, and so it is irrelevant to the point I was making.

WILL: Are you aware that the Epistles of Clement are dated at around 96A.D., a full 66 years after the supposed ascension of Jesus and roughly 26 years after the Gospel of Mark, which I referenced as the first written accounts of Jesus? If one were to assume an author would have at least needed to be over 10 years old to properly recollect something, would that not at least suggest an age of about 76 years old, which would have been highly improbable for that time period? And can you demonstrate that the Gospels that appeared in circulation before the Epistles of Clement did not influence Clement's writings at all?

BRAXTON: I was going the extra mile in providing you with first century extra-biblical evidence for Jesus. You did not originally ask for extra-biblical first-hand evidence of Jesus. You claimed, "In other words there are no existing first-hand accounts of Jesus in existence." However, while I still maintain and have demonstrated (with your data) that first century life expectancy was permitting, I think Paul's first letter to the Corinthian church satisfies. Paul would have had first hand evidence. And The Jesus Seminar doesn't deny the historical data in 1 Corinthians 15.

WILL: Can someone know something to be true, but still be wrong? Many people died because they knew communism to be superior to capitalism, and yet history would seem to suggest that regardless of their faith they were quite wrong. Doesn't that suggest that dying for something does not make it true?

BRAXTON: No, someone can not *know* something to be true and be wrong. This violates the law of non-contradiction. They can, however, believe something to be true and yet be wrong. Communism is not a singular event; it is an ideology, thus the comparison is invalid. For example, it makes no sense for some to say, "Does everyone remember yesterday at 4:00pm when communism happened?"

WILL: Why would you compare something which happened in the 20th century, under the strict control of well trained modern surgeons with the crucifixion, death, 2-3 days of being dead, and being resurrected by angels or god? And how does that respond to the point I was making, that personal, unverifiable experience is immaterial to debate?

BRAXTON: I wouldn't make that comparison, you did. And you didn't ask, "Did Jesus really say that?" (unverified personal claims). You said, "If I had claimed to be god before going into surgery, would I be God?"

WILL: Since it's impossible to use science to suggest that the earth was created in six 24-hour days, why would you suggest that faith does not involve suspending science or reason? Since it's impossible to demonstrate that heaven exists, why would you suggest that faith does not involve suspending science or reason?

BRAXTON: I have not argued here for a six day creation and 6,000 year old earth. I have not argued in this debate for the reality of heaven. I have my own views, but that is not the subject of this debate.

WILL: If the Bible is inaccurate about god slaughtering people, committing genocide, and ordering murders and rapes, why would you assume that the rest of the Bible is accurate? Why would you assume any of the Bible is accurate? Why would you assume the Torah or Qur'an are accurate? Thus why would you assume that theism is accurate?

BRAXTON: I did not say that the Bible was inaccurate on those matters. Nor did I claim that the Bible is accurate on other matters. Once again, I have my own views but as I have not argued on the basis of the biblical testimony (with the exception of 1 Cor. 15 which holds a special place among scholarship), whether the Bible is accurate or not is not the subject of this debate. If you would like to have another debate on that subject I'll be happy to accommodate. All I'm saying is there is no reason to hold me to something I have not argued. However, you then make a broad leap from biblical accuracy to theism. I don't see why Biblical inerrancy is a necessary state (philosophically speaking) for theism to be true.

WILL: If I can demonstrate a way for one religion to begin, why would that way not be possible for another religion? And are you aware that if a genetic fallacy is used in tandem with other evidences and arguments which establish the illogical conclusions of an opponent, it ceases to be a fallacy?

BRAXTON: I didn't say that the way you described would not be possible for Christianity to have begun that way. I am claiming that there is no warrant for thinking so. Moreover, it is certainly not a necessary state. With regard to your comments on the logical fallacy, you haven't demonstrated that your opponent's view is illogical so the fallacy stands. However, it is incorrect that the genetic fallacy would then grant logical justifiability.

WILL: Can you present verifiable studies which explore the reasons people join a religion which include "examination of evidence?" If not, can we agree that this point is not demonstrable because personal experience cannot be verified in this format?

BRAXTON: I was merely responding to your claim that no one comes to Christian belief via evidence. Based on that, the driving point behind your question should be directed at your own comments.

WILL: Is it unreasonable for me to use established science and logic as determining measures for the existence of god or gods? Is my using these measures presupposing naturalism, or is it presupposing verifiable reality?

BRAXTON: On the contrary, I think you have abandoned science and logic at the point of the existence of God. Your refusal to allow those same measurements to be used in these cosmological waters exposes a presupposing of naturalism. It is much like the Richard Lewontin quote, "It is not that the methods and institutions of science somehow compel us to accept a material explanation of the phenomenal world, but, on the contrary, that we are forced by our *a priori* adherence to material causes to create an apparatus of investigation and a set of concepts that produce material explanations, no matter how counter-intuitive, no matter how mystifying to the uninitiated. Moreover, that materialism is an absolute, for we cannot allow a Divine Foot in the door."

WILL'S SECOND REBUTTAL

I didn't criticize your arguments because I've heard them before, I was using them to illustrate the difference between the rules of science/logic and of faith.

I need to clear a few things up. The Big Bang model does not suggest that something came from nothing, or that everything was caused by the Big Bang. According to physicists such as Hawking, existence as we know it expanded from a small, superdense singularity about 13.7b years ago. The Big Bang was the moment of transition from singularity to universe. That singularity, which existed before the Big Bang, is not "nothing" and it is not "god" as it is not sentient or intelligent. Because we know next to nothing about the singularity, we cannot claim with any certainty that it came first. I'm sure you're thinking, "well, eventually we'll get back to a point where something began," but that's not supportable at all. There's no actual rule in science that says, "everything that exists has a cause," or that there's some sort of "first cause." Because of the nature of the singularity, that it was of such a great density and heat, there's no way for us right now to determine it's origin or, assuming it had a cause, what its cause might be. Let me put it in these terms. In theism, the general belief is that god always existed. How, then, would it be a leap for you to believe that the singularity always existed? There's certainly no evidence that the singularity had a beginning.

The "infinite universe theory" states that the universe exists everywhere and for all time. I never made that argument. My argument is that you cannot say with any level of certainty that there was a beginning of existence, which I demonstrated above.

[As far as the *Order* of the universe] You still can't demonstrate the likelihood that it could happen any other way. In order to demonstrate that the universe is fine-tuned, you must demonstrate the probability of it being tuned the way it is and in order to do that, you need to know what the alternatives are and how likely they are. No one has that information, it is unknown, thus assuming god is responsible is god of the gaps.

[As for *Rules* (morality)] Murder is bad for survival, therefore, the people without murderous tendencies survived better, thus to not murder became an innate trait for nearly all societies. Innate moral tendencies are generally normalized throughout every population because our ancestors all went through virtually identical processes of evolution when it comes to murder. Hitler, an extreme case, is an example of social norms, groupthink, and a number of other things overriding innate moral tendencies. All of this is verified by the very best evolutionary biologists or evolutionary sociologists.

Here's what worries me: If Dr. Francis Collins believes in objective morality, what reason would he have to study the evolutionary roots of morality? He wouldn't, thus cutting off an entire area of science from his worldview. The evolutionary roots of ethics is a very active field of study right now, and could use a mind like Dr. Collins', but because of his theistic, religious beliefs he wouldn't be able to reconcile his theism with science. Isaac Newton made the same mistake, believe it or not. Normally, Newton didn't mention god in his writings. When Newton cracked the universal law of gravitation, there was not "and god did this." Why? He understood it. The problem came when Newton was trying to apply the two body problem to the entire solar system, and instead of continuing to create more mathematics in order to explain the stability of the solar system, Newton says: "The six primary planets revolve about the sun in circles concentric with the sun, with the same direction of motion, and very nearly in the same plane . . . This most elegant system of the sun, planets, and comets could not have arisen without the design and dominion of an intelligent and powerful being . . ." That's Isaac Newton, at the end of his knowledge, invoking intelligent design. You know what the sad part of this is? Newton is probably the greatest scientific mind in the history of mankind. He would invent new kinds of calculus for fun. But because he bowed to "God did it," we ended up having to wait for Laplace to figure it out 100 years later. The math Laplace did was not above the level of Newton. Newton probably could have done it in his sleep, but because he bowed to a theological belief instead of a scientific belief, a belief which can be tested and verified, Newton never got to see the beauty of perturbation theory. What if we miss out on that breakthrough in evolutionary genetics because Dr. Collins just accepts the concept that there's an objective morality? That'd be a big disappointment and it would make a very strong case for theism being less reasonable.

[On the resurrection] Please cite specific evidence. You can attribute it to Gary Habermas, but I can't read a whole book as a part of a debate. What do you feel are maybe the three strongest pieces of evidence that Habermas has? I'd like a chance to refute those specifically.

[On the first century extra-biblical sources] You didn't demonstrate it was extra-Biblical, or that it had a source independent of the Gospels.

[On the *Commitment* level of the early church] How many soldiers have put their life on the line and died because they thought that Iraq had something to do with 9/11? Turns out that Iraq had no connections to 9/11, but those soldiers are still quite dead. I don't call that evidence, I'd call it a tragedy. Just like someone willing to die for his or her religion is a tragedy. Anyway, I'm not sure that "if you join our side, we require the kind of belief that could cause you to die" is a good argument for "theism is the more reasonable position."

As your friend said, "If a man claims to be God and rises from the dead we should believe him." I was alive, dead, then alive again. Had I claimed that I was god before this procedure, according to Mike Licona's statement, he would believe me to be god. I would not be god, therefore, the axiom is faulty. Anyway, I have yet to see your positive historical evidence that there was a Jesus, let alone evidence that he rose from the dead.

[On the nature of biblical "faith"] My understanding, like your understanding, comes from my experience in church. I was taught by my father, who was taught by Concordia Seminary, which is the authority on LCMS doctrine. Now you're right that the official stance of the Roman Catholic church (which does not represent all of theism) is that fideism is a thing of the past and that Thomas Aquinas' logic is sound, but that belief isn't necessarily what's taught in the churches. We may have to leave this one.

[On the atheist problem of evil argument] You can't claim that it's a faulty dilemma unless you step up to the plate with an alternative I can respond to. I'm aware of the free will argument, the heaven argument, the "god is beyond logic" cop-out, and the "without evil there is no good" fallacy. If you've got something new, I'd like to get a chance to see it before you simply declare that you're right and I'm wrong.

[On the oppositions point that the inerrancy of Scripture is not the primary focus of the debate] I couldn't disagree with you more. What is theism without religious texts? It's nothing. Christianity and Islam, which constitute the majority of theists in the world, base their theistic beliefs on these texts. If these texts can be demonstrated to be incorrect or in err, the position that theism is reasonable could be called into question.

[On the genetic fallacy] It's only a genetic fallacy if the origin of a thing does not speak to its continuing meaning or context. In this case it very much does. If there is a non-supernatural explanation for the origin of religion, why is the supernatural explanation more correct?

[On former atheist, Anthony Flew] Antony Flew fell into the same trap that got Newton, "god of the gaps." "My one and only piece of relevant evidence [for an Aristotelian God] is the apparent impossibility of providing a naturalistic theory of the origin from DNA of the first reproducing species."—Flew

It's a shame, because we've actually had several wonderful threads about the various current natural hypothesis for abiogenesis on our forum.

I'm not presupposing anything. If provided with evidence for something, I will investigate it honestly and using the metrics of science and logic will come to the best conclusion I'm capable of regardless of my atheism. The fact that I'm unwilling to use supernatural metrics only comes from the fact that I remain unconvinced of the supernatural. You have to bear in mind that because the onus is always on the side of the believer (as no one is born religious). If I find it compelling, the burden has been met. If I find it un-compelling, as I have so far, the burden will not have been met. Anyway, it's not a presupposition, but something in statistics called "null hypothesis."

BRAXTON'S SECOND REBUTTAL

Actually, you did criticize my arguments on the basis of having heard them before. You said, "With all respect, I've seen all of your arguments before, and many, many more." That's fine, I'm just pointing out that the alternative is true.

With regard to the cosmological argument, whether or not the event known as the Big Bang was the beginning or not, you have still not dealt with the impossibility of an infinite regression. Even if there was a chain of Big Bang phenomena that stretch back through history, or even with a singularity, there still would have had to have been an initial point in time. Time would have had to come to exist. Furthermore, you have misstated my arguments. In my first premise I did not state that everything that exists had a cause, I claimed that everything that "begins" to exist must have a cause for its existence. Are you really arguing that the universe did not begin to exist? You claim that there is no law in science that states that everything must have a cause, however, causality is vital to understanding physics. Which is more reasonable, "something caused everything," or "nothing caused everything from nothing?" Certainly in philosophical discussion there are contingent states and necessary states. You asked, "the general belief is that god always existed. How, then, would it be a leap for you to believe that the singularity always existed?" This is a misunderstanding of what we know must be true of the necessary first cause. Whatever came before space-time did not begin to exist because "begin" is a temporal term. Thus, whatever was the necessary first cause of space-time had no beginning to its existence, thus satisfying the term "necessary."

I have demonstrated that the universe must have had a beginning for its existence and you have, even if indirectly, argued for an infinite universe. Immediately following your claim that you do not maintain an infinite universe (with regard to regression since that is what you were responding to), you said, "you cannot say with any level of certainty that there was a beginning of existence." This strikes me as talking in circles.

I have heard no response to my claim that "the greatest probability is that the universe would never have come to exist at all on its own because out of nothing, nothing comes!" You then again invoke the "god of the gaps" argument, but have not dealt with my response to that, stated throughout this debate including my first speech, that whatever caused time, space and matter, must be non-temporal, spaceless and non-material. The cause of those things cannot be made of the caused thing.

Your response regarding Hitler and the societal need to remove murder and genocide may be the point to which we have evolved right now, on your view, but we cannot say that it will be the case in the future. It may be that societal norms change again in the process of moral evolution rendering society's views of genocide to be moral. Thus, far from declaring anything objectively wrong, we cannot even claim rape, murder, pedophilia, racism, genocide or anything else to be definitively wrong. Indeed, wrongness and rightness have no definitive meaning whatsoever on such a view. Your understanding has poor explanatory scope in that it describes a reality that you must then live in contradiction to (or as though it were otherwise). Furthermore, Francis Collins' view is such that societal evolution is not sufficient to explain morality as it is experienced. That *is* his contribution to that field of study. If every time a scientist came to a conclusion that differed from what some of his contemporaries held, [he was then immediately discredited] we would never have arrived at many of our modern advances.

Regarding Habermas, I did not cite any of his arguments, only that he has taken years to count the number of scholars that agree that Jesus actually lived (among other things), and has concluded that the overwhelming majority hold that he did. But, if you don't like Habermas, take agnostic Bob Price who claims that there may be a few authentic sentences here and there, but most of it [the New Testament] was created and compiled by the early church and therefore does not contain much, if any, early witness. Price admits that he is way out there on this one and that very few scholars, even in the liberal camp, would agree with him. If the very man who has made it his primary focus to argue for Jesus' non-existence admits as much, I think we should put it to rest.

You didn't ask me to provide extra-biblical first hand accounts of Jesus, you simply asked for first hand accounts by someone who would have been alive during the time of Christ and I provided you with the one most liberal scholarship agree upon.

You claimed that soldiers who have given their lives in Iraq died for a lie, thus Christians who would have witnessed the resurrected Christ would have also died for a lie. I think the difference is obvious. Soldiers do not live or die based on whether they agree or disagree with every claim of their government. They live or die based on following commanding protocol, love for country, self sacrifice, and a variety of other factors. Christians who knew whether or not Christ had resurrected would not die if they knew Christ had not been resurrected as this was the lynchpin of their belief.

Your comparison of your *near death* experience to Jesus' *death* experience I have already explained. You had, as I said, a *near death* experience, not a *death* experience. However, if you claimed to be God and died, brain cells and all and then rose again three days later, you better believe I would give it a second look. Also, I have posted historical evidence for Jesus and demonstrated that modern scholarship agrees with me. Separate from my C.O.R.E. F.A.C.T.S. argument I must say, that the idea that a common carpenter from the backside of the ancient Near East who never traveled very far from his home, never wrote anything down, and limited his followers during his earthly ministry would 2000+ years later still be the most influential human being in history is impressive enough, but your belief that he never even existed makes it almost as remarkable as the claim that something came from nothing without a necessary cause.

You said we may have to leave the issue of what "faith" is alone. I am fine with that as long as you no longer confine theists (particularly me) to an understanding of that term which is not in keeping with the orthodox position. My heart goes out to you that your church experience developed in you a misconception of what Christian theism has always held on this issue. This passage is not relevant to my argument, but 1 Peter 3:15 actually warns against fideism.

On the "problem of evil," you have presented a faulty dilemma in that you have presupposed that God cannot both exist and evil exist. An assumption has also been made that God's actions should line up with your understanding of morality. Besides the fact that you don't believe morality is objective, your argument rests on the premise that the bad things that happen are bad, or evil. But, as you said there is no objective basis for morality. Terms like good, bad, better, worse, and evil have no real basis. In other words your argument that God allows evil presupposes that there is objective evil.

You claimed, "What is theism without religious texts? It's nothing." I find this to be an amazing statement since throughout this debate I have not referenced Scripture to demonstrate theism one time. In fact, you have quoted more Scripture than I have. It is precisely my contention that one can arrive at theism without any religious texts. However, if you would like to pour a little Scriptural gravy on it, Romans 1:20 says the same claiming, "For since the creation of the world God's invisible qualities—his eternal power and divine nature—have been clearly seen, being understood from what has been made, so that men are without excuse." Now don't misunderstand me to say that I don't view Scripture to be important, just that it is not necessary to establish theism. Since I have not used Scripture in my argumentation for theism it would not mean theism was not true if the Scriptures were never written. This is another faulty dilemma.

With regard to your commission of the genetic fallacy, I do not agree, nor have I seen you demonstrate that Christianity has a naturalistic explanation.

Anthony Flew did not commit the "god of the gaps." He argued the same as you have for decades, and to say he doesn't understand it is untenable. His position is that the complexity that we see in DNA has no naturalistic explanation and is positive evidence of a designer. When positive evidence is introduced for God, the "god of the gaps" argument is no longer on the table.

The null-hypothesis is only active when there is no outstanding evidence to the contrary. I am glad to hear you say that you would be willing to evaluate the evidence and are open to the possibility of God's existence, and I hope that such will be the case.

WILL'S CLOSING REMARKS

By the very own rules of a religious person, god is benevolent, god understands and is aware of evil, god is omnipotent, and god intervenes. I presented the old Epicurean argument. Nothing in it has been disputed other than "it's a false choice," without demonstrating any alternative choice. In the second affirmative rebuttal, it was suggested that I'm not living up to my own beliefs. Of course not, the Epicurean paradox doesn't speak to atheism or skepticism, it seeks to demonstrate that theistic beliefs in god are contradictory, so it follows that each of the rules in the paradox are entirely theistic, including objective morality.

I presented a non-supernatural root for theistic belief that the affirmative even admitted could have been the case. The only argument I got was "nor have I seen you demonstrate that Christianity has a naturalistic explanation." This argument is about theism, not specifically Christianity.

The final point was a question of the very legitimacy of the other side as it violates it's own rules in debating at all. The argument against my point was that one church body doesn't accept that officially. That doesn't really demonstrate anything, though. The church is officially against many things it actually endorses. "Christianity has historically maintained that its adherents have trust (faith) in what God will do in the future based on what we can demonstrate happened in the past." That's not the definition of faith.

Faith:

1 a : allegiance to duty or a person : loyalty b (1) : fidelity to one's promises (2) : sincerity of intentions
2 a (1) : belief and trust in and loyalty to God (2) : belief in the traditional doctrines of a religion b (1) : firm belief in something for which there is no proof (2) : complete trust
3 : something that is believed especially with strong conviction; especially : a system of religious beliefs (the Protestant faith)

The only reference to evidence is one definition that describes faith as "firm belief in something for which there is no proof." Either faith is the wrong word used in every church in the world, or the faith I described is more correct than the affirmative is willing to admit.

All of my points stand. There is an entirely non-supernatural explanation for the existence of religion and theism, theism is contradictory by its very nature, and arguing the side of theism violates theistic rules. I would suggest, based on these, that theism cannot be the more reasonable position. Thanks.

BRAXTON'S CLOSING REMARKS

In my closing remarks I'd like to point out some of the interesting themes of this debate and mention some of the conclusions we are justifiably warranted in arriving at based on C.O.R.E. F.A.C.T.S.

Will has mentioned the "problem of evil" argument and relied almost exclusively on it throughout the duration of this debate. However, this argument is understood by philosophy to commit the fallacy of the "faulty dilemma." He claims that I have not offered an alternative, but he himself mentioned several alternative possibilities argued by theists today. So long as even one of those arguments is even remotely possible, a philosophical "defeater" has been established and the "faulty dilemma" stands. Moreover, this argument assumes attributes of God that are not necessary for theism to be true.

He argues that his naturalistic explanation for how theism could have developed is sufficient to answer theism, but not Christianity. Fine, but if Christianity is true, then theism is true. Moreover, such an explanation may be "sufficient" to explain how theistic ideas developed, but it is not "necessary" for theism to have developed. Even worse, it is insufficient to explain the cosmological, teleological and other C.O.R.E. arguments I put forth. In short, it doesn't get the job done.

Will has claimed that theism demands that theists do not debate their position. Based on what? I see absolutely no basis for such a claim.

He argues that "faith," based on Webster's dictionary, does not allow for the orthodox position. So what? The etymological use of faith among theists need not match the modern western understanding, and more importantly, from a Christian perspective, Will never dealt with my Scriptural passages that demonstrate that Christianity has always argued against fideism.

He has misrepresented, sidestepped and in some cases ignored the Kalam cosmological argument. He has used straw man arguments repeatedly, arguing against a young earth model, six day creation model, the inerrancy of Scripture and holding me to a definition of faith to which I do not subscribe.

We have heard no answer to the infinite regression, nor the necessary attributes of the first cause, which taken alone makes theism more reasonable.

With regard to objective morality we have only heard a rejection of the work of one of the greatest minds in modern day genetics, Francis Collins.

Rather than dealing with the death and resurrection of Jesus, we have heard the fringe hypothesis that the most influential individual in human history never existed.

And we have heard rhetorical claims that no individual has come to faith based on the veracity of apologetic evidence; something that I know is untrue of some viewing this debate.

Since these arguments, particularly the cosmological, have not been answered, I think it is much more reasonable to accept theism than atheism.

Since these will be the final official comments of this debate, I want to say a final word. I really, really do appreciate your tone, Will. You have been cordial at least and respectful at best. I find it interesting that you and I share such a similar background. We both had fathers who were Christian pastors, we were both raised in a Christian home, and we both have a passion for getting at the truth. It breaks my heart to hear that what led you to a rejection of theism was the idea that the faithful doubt. Surely, you have doubted your atheism. Doubt is healthy. I sometimes doubt my wife's love, but this does not mean I am not married. We have both studied greatly the evidence and read some of the same books. The only difference is that I concluded that theism was correct and you concluded atheism. Since I am done debating, I want to make a sincere invitation to everyone here. God does exist. He cares about all of you. He created the very atoms that comprise your body. As the Father, he exists outside of the material universe, as the Son he entered it and died that you might transcend it, and as the Spirit, he makes such a connection possible. I would invite each of you, if only in your private moments, to trust him based on what we know he has done in the past, that he will do what he claims in the future.

Thanks so much.

ABOUT THE AUTHOR

Braxton Hunter is Professor of Christian Apologetics at Trinity College of the Bible and Theological Seminary in Newburgh, Indiana. He is the former President of the Conference of Southern Baptist Evangelists, and is the Director of Evangelism for Trinity Crusades for Christ. Dr. Hunter holds a B.A. in Expository Preaching, an M.A. in Theology and a Ph.D. in Christian Apologetics.